KNOW
BETTER
TO DO
BETTER

Also by Denny Emerson

How Good Riders Get Good

KNOW BETTER TO DO BETTER

Mistakes I Made with Horses
(So You Don't Have To)

■■■

Denny Emerson

Trafalgar Square
North Pomfret, Vermont

First published in 2018 by
Trafalgar Square Books
North Pomfret, Vermont 05053

Disclaimer of Liability

The author and publisher shall have neither liability nor responsibility to any person or entity with respect to any loss or damage caused or alleged to be caused directly or indirectly by the information contained in this book. While the book is as accurate as the author can make it, there may be errors, omissions, and inaccuracies.

Trafalgar Square Books encourages the use of approved safety helmets in all equestrian sports and activities.

The author and publisher have made every effort to obtain a release from photographers whose images appear in this book. In some cases, however, the photographers were not known or could not be contacted. Should additional photographers be identified, they will be credited in future editions of this book.

ISBN: 978 1 57076 895 8
Library of Congress Control Number: 2018036066

All photographs courtesy of the author except: p. 8 (by Al Kania); p. 9 (courtesy of Judy Richter); p. 31 (by Stacy Holmes); pp. 36, 52 (courtesy of Lefreda Williams); pp. 42, 192, 213 (by Nick Goldsmith Photography); p. 49 (courtesy of Kathy Livingston); p. 53 (by Cindy Arendt); p. 81 (by Rhett Savoie); p. 116 (by Cora Cushny); p. 138 (by JPL Photography); p. 197 (by Genie Stewart-Spears); p. 198 (by Fifi Coles)
Book design by Lauryl Eddlemon
Cover design by RM Didier
Index by Andrea M. Jones (www.jonesliteraryservice.com)

Typefaces: Avenir, Droid Serif

Printed in China

10 9 8 7 6 5 4 3 2 1

Dedication

■ ■ ■

**To five friends for more than 60 years,
as obsessed with horses as I am (maybe
more so!): Judy Cameron Barwood,
Allen Leslie, Nancy Ela Caisse,
Jeannine Kraus Myers, and Ted Niboli.
It's been quite a ride.**

■ ■ ■

Contents

Introduction

There are already hundreds of books about horses. Some of them tell stories of fictitious horses and the people around them while others tell about real horses that performed great feats of athletic valor.

Some horse books teach you how to ride in a specific way. Others describe how to train horses to perform better in various riding or driving disciplines. Some talk about the characteristics of a particular breed of horse or pony. Others teach you about feeding, shoeing, tack selection, trailering, how to lay out a farm, how to braid, how to groom, how to lead a foal, how to breed a winning racehorse—the list of books goes on and on and on.

Some of these books are light reading, meant to entertain, even if they do not always adhere closely to the way it actually works with real horses and real people.

Some are meant to teach. Of the teaching books, I have found some to be full of superb advice but so ponderously written as to be akin to studying a textbook on organic chemistry. Others, fortunately, are easier to read.

There is no such thing as a horse book that will be all things to all people. The world of horses is too diverse, too wide, too deep, and too all-encompassing for any one book to begin to cover it all in anything but a surface brush-over.

So why should I presume to add another book to a vast and constantly growing library?

Good question, but here is why I think that *Know Better to Do Better* might be a useful addition.

My Own Path to Learning

I started out at 10 years old literally as "backyard" as backyard gets. When my parents succumbed to my pleading for a pony, and Paint (see sidebar) was about to be delivered, I took loads of junk out of an old chicken coop in the backyard of the house that we lived in on Bernardston Road, in Greenfield, Massachusetts, so it could be Paint's stall when he wasn't living out in a field.

The sum total of my knowledge about horses came from cowboy radio shows, cowboy comic books, cowboys and Indians movies, and whatever I'd learned by osmosis from being a barn rat at the Stoneleigh-Prospect Hill School, a 20-second walk from our back door.

Over the following 67 years, I did lots of things with lots of horses in all kinds of riding disciplines, and much of this was through trial and error—the classic "school of hard knocks"—especially at the beginning.

Later, as I got to be more "famous," and rode on a gold-medal winning team for the United States Equestrian Team, doors of instruction opened that had formerly been locked shut.

My own path to learning, in other words, started at ground zero, and zigzagged, over decades, through hundreds of horses of many different breeds and types and sizes, doing all sorts of riding, starting with gymkhanas in a Western saddle or bareback, to saddle seat, to Morgans, to Thoroughbreds, to eventing, dressage, show jumping, competitive trail riding, endurance racing, breeding, standing stallions, a little bit of polo, a little bit of racing, a fair bit of running horse organizations, teaching, doing hundreds of clinics for 40 years, dealing with hundreds and hundreds of riders and horses, trying to figure out ways to help them get to be more successful.

This book is set up with six different headings, or sections, which I call "Horse Selection," "Horse Management," "Horse Training," "A Rider's Emotional Makeup and Character Traits," "A Rider's Physical Skills," and "Rider

Knowledge." Under each heading, there are lots of subsections that focus on various issues and situations from all sorts of perspectives.

I don't think of this book as a story with a beginning, middle, and end. I don't think of it as a "teach-me-how-to-ride" book, nor as a "how-do-I-get-the-best-horse-for-me" book. It's all of these and more, based on my decades of watching the triumphs and mistakes of many of the world's greatest riders, riding some of the finest horses. It is from watching some of the most novice riders in the world struggling with horses that scare and hurt them. It is from my own mistakes and wrong perceptions and, sometimes, my winning breakthroughs, by which I don't necessarily mean winning blue ribbons or gold medals. There was some of that, of course, but I mean winning in the greater sense, by doing things that were right for my horses, and starting to finally learn right from wrong, for their sake.

> My winning break-throughs over the years weren't necessarily winning blue ribbons or gold medals. They were mostly about winning in the greater sense, by doing things that were right for my horses, and starting to finally learn right from wrong, for their sake.
>
> ◼ ◼ ◼

Certainly, many of the references I have used in the pages ahead pertain to eventing, because that was a main focus that I had for many decades. The relevant fact about eventing, though, is that within one riding discipline are so many requirements and spillovers from other parts of the greater horse world mosaic.

At its heart, when it is done correctly, eventing is about horse health, horse fitness, horse physical soundness, and horse mental and emotional stability.

Eventing also encapsulates dressage training, up to a reasonably high level, show-jumping techniques, which at eventing's Advanced level become reasonably challenging, gymnastics, galloping, and maintaining a program that can mesh these disparate tasks without confusing or subjugating the horse.

But in addition to eventing, I was involved in Western riding and gymkhanas as a kid, in horse breeding, endurance racing, fox hunting, competitive trail, rehoming and reschooling OTTBs (Off-the-Track Thoroughbreds), showing Morgans, showing in straight dressage, show jumping and hunters, judging at

Paint

I got lucky with my first pony, because Paint was a quiet, tolerant pony who forgave my worst mistakes.

Plato said, "For things which we must learn before we can do them, we learn by doing them." That pertains to so many things, like how a baby learns to walk and to talk. It allows and sees as inevitable so much failure, so many mistakes, and so much trial and error, and that is what Paint allowed me.

When I got him in the fall of 1952, I had just turned 11, and I had only ridden a few times on some of the Stoneleigh-Prospect Hill School horses, not enough to have learned anything. I was small and ignorant, but Paint was also small, maybe 14 hands or 14.1, and tolerant, and I just climbed on and rode, no lessons, just learning by doing.

I had a Western saddle, but mainly I rode bareback. I'd watched enough Westerns at the two Greenfield movie theaters to know that Indians could mount by leaping up and throwing their right leg over the pony's back, and Paint was short enough so that I could do

"A kid-broke hoss" was how Louis Goodyear described Paint to my parents on the day in 1952 that they bought him for me. He was the perfect first pony: steady, quiet, and tolerant of my beginner mistakes. I could not have been luckier.

that. He lived in a big field and he wore a halter. I took a normal lead rope with a snap on one end, and I wired a snap to the other end to make a set of reins.

I would get home from Four Corners School, from fifth and sixth grade, grab my lead rope, catch Paint from the pasture, hitch a snap on the right and left ring of his halter, leap up and off I would go exploring the woods to the north of the campus. I was learning to ride the old-fashioned way, not by getting riding lessons, but just by riding. Pretty soon I could walk, trot, canter and gallop like those little Indian kids, uphill, downhill, just by balance and 11- and 12-year-old agility.

In April of 1954, when I was 12, I entered Paint in five or six classes at the Stoneleigh gymkhana—events like pole bending, musical sacks, break-the-balloon, egg-and-spoon, and sit-a-buck— and I won my very first class of my very first riding competition. I won a couple of other classes, and at the end of the gymkhana, one of the "big" Stoneleigh girls saw me flaunting my ribbons on Paint's bridle, and she said, "Beginner's luck."

I've heard plenty of people say things like, "My first pony was a dirty, rotten scoundrel. He bucked me off at least once a week, and that pony was the making of me as a tough, competent rider." And so forth.

Well, maybe so. But if I had to guess, I would say that for every child who gets to be tough and fearless because of having that classic "rotten pony," there are many more who get put off riding forever. Either because they got scared, or they got hurt, or they just got frus-trated by the endless struggle.

Give me a quiet and forgiving pony or horse like Paint any day of the week over a tough little rat. As I said, I was lucky to have him for my first teacher.

In Retrospect: What I'd Do Differently with Paint

Looking back to 1952 from 2018, there isn't much that I would change. Most good horse people will tell you that the first horse or pony should have the temperament that allows the green or young rider to get away with making every mistake in the book, and Paint did that for me.

Louis Goodyear, the dealer in Sunderland, Massachusetts, knew what I needed, and he made sure to steer me toward what he called "a kid-broke hoss." Louis was one of those savvy old-time horsemen, and it only took him a couple of minutes watching a kid ride to size up what kind of horse would suit, and he just didn't bring out the wrong ones for you to try.

So, I guess you could say that by steering me toward Paint, Louis prevented me from ever needing a "do-over button" with Paint, and what a gift that was.

such shows as the Royal Dublin Show in Ireland, as well as getting involved at a high level with the administration of a number of American horse associations.

The point being that this book, I think, comes at problems and strategies and training objectives from a number of angles and from a number of perspectives, so that I hope it can be useful and relevant to riders from all sorts of backgrounds.

A Tool Box for Horse Owners, Riders, and Trainers

When my publishers and I were first thinking of a title for this book, one suggestion was, "Why Didn't They Tell Me That?" Another idea was "Mistakes I Made So You Don't Have To." This book is both of these, and, I hope, a lot more. I hope that it can be as simple as a useful "tool box" of ideas that a reader can refer to when in need of solutions or ideas, sort of the way most people have cookbooks in their kitchen. They don't read them every day, but when the time comes to make a casserole, it's handy to have the recipe at hand.

There will be some redundancies, and they are deliberate. In my own learning, I've found that hearing something again in a slightly different way enables me to suddenly "get it," and so I've tried to come at things from different angles.

> I hope this book will help riders and trainers and horse owners discover what it took me so many years of zigs and zags, false starts, and mistakes to finally begin to learn.
>
> ■ ■ ■

I hope this book will also help riders and trainers and horse owners discover what it took me so many years of zigs and zags, false starts, and mistakes to finally begin to learn, which when coming right down to it, is pretty darn simple.

Horses are a species of animal entirely vulnerable to and dependent upon the humans who control their lives and destinies. Do we humans do right by them, or do we cause them anxiety, discomfort, and pain? If we conclude that, as horse people, our goal is to make their lives better, then what we do on a daily basis is the key to making that happen.

This is why I wrote this book.

1

Horse Selection

Fandom Rules the Horse World— and Leads to Discipline and Breed Preference

There must be something buried in the human psyche that craves an object of blind devotion, else why would there be fans of anything? Think about it. A 10-year-old boy, typical in many respects, is blindly obsessed with baseball, say, the New York Yankees, and football, the New England Patriots. Now this kid has never met an actual Yankee or Patriot and probably never will. But if you want to start an argument that has no end, say something demeaning about either team and you will hear a vast litany of reasons why these two teams, and these alone, are superior to all others.

Political parties, religions, nationalities, hobbies, and brands of cars all have their champions (and their detractors), and often there isn't much logic, analytical thinking, or empirical evidence underlying these obsessions.

It's no different in the large world of horses. Try telling a devotee of some particular breed that some other breed is better and you are right there arguing with that 10-year-old about the relative merits of the Yankees versus the Red Sox, with no hope of either party convincing the other in 10,000 years.

You may be an obsessed dressage rider, but you'll be highly unlikely to ever convince a barrel racer to switch disciplines.

Most of the horse breeds and the horse disciplines have entire subcultures surrounding them, with associations, magazines, websites, blogs, registries, and competitive venues in interlocking webs of support. Once you have decided to pick one and choose to become (pick one: a show jumper, an eventer, a trail rider) riding (pick one: a Thoroughbred, a Morgan, a Paint), there is an entire network created and designed to make you feel comfortable and part of something special and larger and more important than yourself.

The Hofmanns

I n both direct and indirect ways, one of the families that has influenced my path as a rider, author, and volunteer for various horse organizations has been the Hofmann family from New Jersey and Vermont, Mr. and Mrs. Hofmann (Philip and Mary), and their two superbly gifted daughters, Carol Hofmann Thompson and Judy Hofmann Richter.

Mr. Hofmann was the first president and a founding member of the United States Eventing Association. Both Mr. and Mrs. Hofmann were instrumental in keeping the Green Mountain Horse Asso-

Mary Hofmann presenting an award to me and Cat. She was a stalwart supporter of the Green Mountain Horse Association in South Woodstock, Vermont, back in the day when the organization (now extremely popular) was struggling.

There are enormous gulfs separating these segments of the equestrian world. Arabian lovers will not be found at an Appaloosa show, nor reiners at the Grand Prix of Aachen. Drivers drive, steeplechase jockeys steeplechase, Western riders ride in saddles with saddle horns, and show jumpers and hunt seat riders do interact but are rarely seen at any type of trail ride. There are a few areas of commonality, like the quest for veterinary advances, or the need for good hay or trailers, but basically, there's little to bind the disparate elements together.

The main problem with blind devotion to anything is that it tends to rule out all kinds of opportunities that are available to those with vision. Here's just

ciation in South Woodstock, Vermont, alive and well during the 1950s and 1960s.

Carol, who died recently, far too soon, was the picture of classical elegance over fences, a consummate role model.

But it has been Judy Hofmann Richter who has helped me the most, as a riding role model, as an advocate of classical teaching, and as a supporter of my writing.

The horse industry has been called "a vast mosaic" of interlocking humans, riding styles, breeds, horses, and disciplines. Every now and then, one of the thousands of pieces that combine to create the mosaic will exert a disproportionately positive impact on the overall pattern. The Hofmann family has been an example of that.

Judy Hofmann Richter on Freedom in 1966. She is showing an exemplary position and style on a lovely horse.

one example: Take a young event rider. Let her spend a few years developing her eventing base. Then let her spend a year in Germany working at a dressage training center. And let her gallop timber horses for an entire year for noted steeplechase trainer, Jonathan Sheppard. Afterward, she should spend a year with world-champion endurance rider Valarie Kanavy. The next year she's back in Europe with a grand prix jumper stable.

Now send her back into eventing, and if she isn't wildly more proficient than when she left four years earlier, she must have spent those opportunities in a drug-induced coma.

Now, nobody I know has done that "total immersion thing" to the extent of my hypothetical example, but there are pieces of that puzzle available to those who are enterprising enough to seek them out. Basically, it's a big, diverse world out there, and if you allow your fandom mindset to limit you, you can bet you'll be surpassed by those more open minded. Hey, we know you're basically whacked, just as most of us can admit that we are similarly "out there." Don't worry. You can crawl back to the secure little nest of the Patriots and the Yankees, and live there happily ever after, but maybe just try some other brands of ice cream before you eat only maple walnut for the rest of your life!

Choosing the Horse

People buy horses for all kinds of reasons and for all manner of intended purposes.

Some buying decisions are strictly analytical, based on bloodlines and performance history, with a clear eye on the bottom line. Others are purely emotional, random, and spur-of-the-moment, based on whim, daydream, and hope (fig. 1.1).

I sometimes think that a good outcome is as likely (or unlikely) using either approach, horses being horses, but there are guidelines and caveats and

decision-making processes that it makes sense not to ignore. In the following discussions, you can look at many of these.

Probably the first consideration is to ask yourself, "What am I going to do with this horse, if I decide to buy him?" Do you just want to look at him standing in a stall or pasture? Do you intend to breed the horse if she is a mare, or are you hoping to ride or drive?

If your goal is to have a riding horse, then what kind of riding do you hope to do? Do you ride English or Western? Is there a specific type of riding sport or discipline that you want to pursue? Does the horse need to be of some specific breed?

The more questions you ask and answer before you jump feet first into a horse purchase, the more likely you will make a wise buying choice rather than one you'll regret.

For most prospective buyers, a big consideration is the purchase price. I know plenty of people who would struggle to pay even $2,000 to $3,000 for a horse. So if this is your situation, it leads to another question.

"Can I afford to keep a horse?" Have you analyzed what it will cost you for horse board, veterinary expenses, shoeing, hay, grain, bedding, transportation, tack, and all the hidden as well as the more obvious pieces of the larger economic puzzle? So many people jump into horse ownership without figuring out whether they can really afford to do it.

The more questions you ask and answer before you jump feet first into a horse purchase, the more likely you will make a wise buying choice rather than one you'll regret.

■ ■ ■

Another big question, and this is one that almost nobody wants to face, is, "What do I do if this horse gets injured to the point that he can no longer be ridden or driven?" Will you keep him "forever" until he dies of old age? Will you have him euthanized? Will you hope to give him away, so that someone else is faced with these hard questions?

And what are you going to do if you buy one that, for whatever reason, apart from unsoundness, makes him unsuitable for you? Will you sell him? Can you afford to keep this one for a pet and still be able to afford another one to be your riding horse?

More questions: Is this going to be a pleasure horse that you ride for fun or do you have competitive riding goals? If you do hope to compete, will this be at a relatively low-key local level, or are you thinking of national or even the international level?

Will this be an "until-death-do-us-part" horse, or are you looking at a horse for where you are in your personal skill level, realizing that he may suit you right now, but be inadequate for your needs as your riding improves and progresses?

Truly, there are so many questions, and although you can't know the future, and while plans and goals may change, the more questions you answer now, even if the answers are only half-formed, the better chance you have of buying the right horse. Many people plunge into horse ownership without first asking all these hard questions, and then, when things go badly wrong, find themselves hopelessly floundering both emotionally and financially.

So, as you read through all the ideas, suggestions and advice in this section of *Know Better to Do Better,* I hope that something will help you in your decision-making process.

Straight Talk About Horse Temperament

Everybody starts out as a beginner. Some people swiftly catch on and get more balanced and comfortable on the back of a moving horse, while others take longer. Some are more innately confident than others. When you have a confident rider, who is also athletically fit, strong, and agile, sure, this rider can get away with having a little more horse perhaps, and won't get scared or tight if the horse is less than steady.

But for many beginning riders, riding a horse that is "up" and reactive is like teaching a kid to ride a bike on a steep, rocky mountain trail: one fall, the kid gets hurt and loses confidence.

You watch riders who are scared, or at any rate, "anxious," and you do not see relaxed and supple hands and arms, but tight, defensive hands (fig. 1.2). The already reactive horse feels the tension in the rider and becomes even more tense, which starts the snowball rolling.

1.2: There are "bad hands, good hands, and educated hands," says George Morris. Bad hands are rough and unfeeling, good hands are sympathetic, while educated hands are like finely tuned instruments, "playing" the mouth, jaw, and poll like the strings of a violin. As can be seen in this photo, the word "hands" can, when communicating with the mouth, jaw, and poll of a horse, include flexible fingers and wrists, even elbows and shoulders. "Hands" is a slight misnomer for something this complex.

On a Scale of One to Ten

If a hot horse is considered a 10, and a lethargic horse a 1, then horses that are 1 to 4 absorb the mistakes of the rider, and horses that are 5 and 6, within reason, tolerate the rider's mistakes, while a horse that's 7 or higher magnifies those mistakes.

Any true horse person understands that beginners, by and large, need steady horses at first, so that they can "get away" with their beginner mistakes without setting off the horse. This allows the beginner to gain confidence and start acquiring various riding skills so, at some point, no longer a beginner, the rider is ready to take on the challenge of a "higher-octane" type of horse. But face reality: Many riders never get all that confident or skilled. Many riders are not all that fit or athletic. Some are recovering from illness or injury. Some start riding as older adults. There are many riders who, if they had access to nice 3–4–5 temperament horses, would be happy and able to ride with success and enjoyment. And we see plenty of these great horse-and-rider matchups.

> How to persuade riders who are not having fun to trade horses for one they could take pleasure in, is one of the great challenges of the entire horse industry, and it often seems to defy solution.
>
> ■ ■ ■

But we also see lots of nervous, tense, anxious, even downright scared riders, knuckles white with tension, jaws clenched in apprehension, trying to ride horses that are what in the trade we call "too much horse" for their situation. These riders would be just fine on lower-scale horses, but not on the horses that magnify their mistakes.

How to persuade riders who are not having fun to trade horses for one they could take pleasure in is one of the great challenges of the entire horse industry, and it often seems to defy solution.

Another Point About Temperament

Let's say your goal is to have a "perfect" 5½.

It is generally one heck of a lot easier to take a 3½ and move him *up*, so he rides like a 5½, than to take a 7½ and move him *down* so he rides like a 5½.

When in doubt, it's better to start *under*-horsed than *over*-horsed.

People ignore this. They would rather "visualize" themselves on a Secretariat than on a Steady-Eddie "Dobbin," so they buy the horse they wish they *could* ride rather than the horse they *can* ride, and start yet another "misery trail" for both horse and rider.

And do you think they will realize that they need a different horse, to the point that they change horses? If you think that, you have not been in the horse game for very long!

Know What You're Looking For

Here are some of the subjects that may or may not be included in your particular list of qualities:

1. Breed: Does this horse have to be, say, a Quarter Horse? If your goal is to compete in Quarter Horse shows, then it obviously must be.

2. Soundness: How sound does this horse have to be to suit your purposes? A beginner horse to learn on may not have to be as sound as the Kentucky Three-Day horse, but that's your decision about how much risk you are willing to take, in consultation with a veterinarian.

3. Temperament: How much "octane in the tank" are you competent to deal with? Be careful! Hot horses tend not to get less hot, and most of us can't ride hot horses with high levels of success. Calm horses tolerate our mistakes, as we learn. The temperament issue is key.

4. Athleticism: If, realistically, you'll be jumping 2 feet 6 inches for the foreseeable future, does this horse have to be able to jump 4 feet 6 inches?

5. Price range: Maybe this should come first, for many buyers.

6. Size: Big riders can often successfully ride small horses, and small riders can ride big ones, so get a sense of what *you* think is okay.

7. Age: Think through the various ramifications of this one.

8. Color: It may not matter one bit, or, say, to a Palomino lover, it may be crucial.

9. "Pretty": How much does this matter? It's a very personal choice.

10. Mare, gelding, or stallion: This matters hugely to some, little to others. Gelding an older stallion has some risks attached.

11. Training: Green, totally schooled, somewhere in between.

The point is to try to figure out in advance what this horse should theoretically possess, knowing that you will almost never get everything that the list contains in one horse.

Horse Breeds

Thoroughbreds

The Thoroughbred is a breed of horse created primarily in England in the seventeenth and eighteenth centuries for racing. This was accomplished by mixing desert-bred stallions of Arabian, Barb, and Tukoman breeding with native mares.

Today, Thoroughbred breeding forms a multi-billion dollar industry, which is still aimed almost exclusively for producing horses to race. It is simply a fortunate happenstance that many of the qualities of the racehorse are also appropriate for the modern sport horse so that when Thoroughbreds finish their racing career, many find a second life in such disciplines as hunters, jumpers, polo, eventing, and even distance riding.

1.3: Bred to be a racehorse, Rosie's Girl failed in that role. Retrained, she has become an upper-level event horse with Daryl Kinney.

Off-the-Track Thoroughbreds (OTTBs)

It is important to realize how intrinsic the idea of betting is to the development of the racehorse, because so much of the fallout and so many of the abuses are directly tied to what happens to the racehorse when it can no longer suit the needs of the gambler (fig. 1.3).

As long as a horse is sound enough to enter the starting gate, and as long as the horse still has at least an outside chance of winning a check, the racing industry has a use for that horse. Once the horse becomes lame or loses its will to try or its physical ability to be competitive, it becomes useless at the racetrack because it can no longer be bet on.

The OTTBs: Affordable and Available

Rosie's Girl with Darryl Kinney schooling over an oxer.

t would be naive and unrealistic to think that dressage riders with upper-level aspirations are going to go out and get an OTTB as their horse of choice, instead of buying a custom-bred dressage Warmblood that came out of the womb floating above the ground, with collection and extension as genetically instilled abilities.

That said, for those who want to build up to becoming good dressage riders, and who want to spend, say, $5,000 or less as they begin that long road to excellence, or for those riders who are happy at somewhat lower than the FEI levels, a nice Thoroughbred can be either a stepping stone or a final partner.

I also think that riders who can take young Thoroughbreds off the track, and who subsequently learn how to train them to be competent dressage horses, can, on a low budget, hone their own riding and training skills so that if that "big" horse comes along, they will be ready to ride it.

This is also true about using the OTTB in distance riding, in show jumping, in eventing, in show hunters. The key thing to realize about the OTTB is that I/you/we/they can buy quite a lot of athlete for quite a low sum of money, often for far less than what it costs to ship a horse from Europe, never mind the cost of buying the horse. And, especially in eventing, sometimes that Thoroughbred can become as elite as any other custom-bred horse available.

When I hear or read about people complaining about how only the very wealthy riders have a shot these days, I think those riders don't "get" the difference between becoming good riders and becoming successful competitors. Yes, the "rich kids" and sponsored riders, on horses that cost as much as many nice farms, they are absolutely going to beat you most every time on your $1,500 to $7,500 OTTB.

Nathan Merchant on his six-year-old OTTB Papa Choo Choo, schooling dressage.

I'm riding Union Station in a North Carolina horse trials.

But:

You can learn to sit the trot and canter with or without stirrups on your affordable OTTB, can you not?

You can learn to see a distance on him, can you not?

You can learn how to put him "on the aids," can you not?

You can learn how to create an adjustable canter on him, can you not?

You can learn how to have lovely posture, either on the flat or over fences, on your OTTB, can you not?

You can log in plenty of mileage over fences or in a dressage ring at shows, while you learn how to get used to performing under pressure on him, can you not?

To say that you cannot learn to become an elite rider on an inexpensive and widely available OTTB is simply and absolutely not true. To say that you *can't*— that is just a cop out.

So, if it so transpires that your grandfather did not have the good grace to start the Amalgamated Widget company, thus leaving you with the necessary trust fund to buy excellence, and you need to become highly skilled another way so that sponsors will want to help you, that other avenue is out there in bay and chestnut and gray and brown as you read this: beautiful, classically bred young Thoroughbreds, as good as ever, are waiting to become your partner on your journey.

Many of us did exactly that, which is why we know that it can be done.

If the horse is a well-bred mare or stallion, it may be used to breed future racehorses, but if the horse is not well bred, it did not race with success, or if it is a gelding, the racing industry has zero further use for it.

The former racehorse that is not destined to be used for breeding is in some ways worse to own than not owning any horse at all, because instead of being a potential income producer, it now becomes an income liability, because it still needs to be fed and housed and given at least minimal care.

I am not talking here about the myths, or the happy ending stories, or the Walt Disney conclusions, but about the stark, hard, economic realities that face used-up racehorses, especially those that are injured in some way.

> I know plenty of success stories, but I know as many stories of failure and heartache about taking on the challenge of turning the former racehorse into a nice riding horse. Don't leap blindly.
>
> ■ ■ ■

These horses were bred and trained for one thing alone—to race for purses—and these purses were made possible by the human need and passion to gamble. That's it. You need to grasp that reality, because it's the base cause behind the problem of what is to become of so many unwanted horses.

So let's consider a lame three-year-old Thoroughbred gelding. I can tell you this right up front—there are not enough pastures in the world owned by enough people with enough money to provide long-term homes for permanently unsound horses. Most of these horses are going to die.

If you can't stand to read this, skip this part. I am not writing this for shock value or to create a crusade, but so that people can understand the realities, and not blindly buy into the feel-good stories that hide the truth.

In recent years, there has been a response by the racing industry to the bad press that was beginning to build up around the issue of so many former racehorses ending up in the so-called "kill pens" at livestock auctions. Those horses would go to slaughterhouses, and their meat would either become pet food or be shipped abroad to countries that do not have our taboo about eating horseflesh.

I suspect that one of the reasons that for so many years there was little response from the racing industry to these stark realities is that oh-so-human tendency to play ostrich, as if by sticking their collective heads in the sand and not seeing the problem, they'd find that the problem didn't really exist.

These days, though, there's lots of support to create safety-net systems to guide former racehorses toward second careers as sport horses. There are dozens, probably hundreds of organizations that take OTTBs, let them down, start them in basic schooling, and try to find them second homes. If you Google "retired racehorse" or "OTTB aftercare," or "retraining Thoroughbred racehorses," you will find more information than you can possibly assimilate.

I know plenty of success stories, but I know as many stories of failure and heartache about taking on the challenge of turning the former racehorse into a nice riding horse. Don't leap blindly. Know what you are getting into. It may be precisely what you need, but it may just as readily be a disaster waiting to happen. So think this through with your intellect, instead of "following your heart." Decisions based on emotion can work, sure, but don't assume a happy ending.

First, the Cons

The very first thing to assess with the help of a veterinarian is whether or not the horse is sound enough to perform or to do the job you want. The former racehorse may never be sound enough to become a useful sport horse. A young horse, galloping at top speed, can get all kinds of injuries, and while some of those injuries can heal over time, there are others that don't.

Even though the young horse that you are considering may cost less than the price of a pre-purchase veterinary exam, it makes so much more sense to pay for the exam than to wind up with a cripple you can't ride, because if that happens, then what?

Are you going to spend several thousand dollars a year for some indeterminate number of years to maintain what is often called a "pasture ornament?" Are you going to have the unsound horse euthanized? What? Be smart. Get a thorough pre-purchase exam. But even if your new horse passes physically, how about his mental and emotional state after the rigors of racing? Some will be as laidback as an old Quarter Horse gelding, but others may be smoking hot. Do you want to deal with smoking hot?

I think that many riders plunge into OTTB ownership without first planning an exit strategy when the dream turns into a nightmare. This can happen with any horse purchase, not only with an OTTB, but I think there often exists a greater degree of uncertainty with a horse that may have already faced hard times on the racetrack.

The Pros, Perhaps

One of the great allures of buying an OTTB is that you may be getting a hugely elite athlete for a fraction of the amount of money put into him to bring him to this point. If you find a lovely, sound, sane four-, five- or six-year-old, someone will have spent thousands of dollars to breed him and train him, and here you are perhaps paying $7,500, or $5,000, or even much less.

Another thing history has taught us is that Thoroughbreds can become hunters, jumpers, event horses, polo ponies, even dressage horses, capable of competing at the highest competitive levels (fig. 1.4).

Discard the stereotype that OTTBs are usually hot. Some are, many are not.

■ ■ ■

Joe Fargis and Bill Steinkraus won Olympic show jumping gold medals on Touch of Class and Snowbound. Bruce Davidson won the 1978 World Championship Three-Day Eventing on Might Tango. Tad Coffin won eventing's 1976 Olympic gold medal on Bally Cor. These are only a few examples, and there are hundreds of others. Thoroughbreds are mega-athletes, and not just for racing.

All that said, what I know is that no matter what advice someone may get, that person will usually do what he or she wants to do. It reminds me of the lines from a song in the musical *My Fair Lady,* "She will beg you for advice,

1.4: Prompt Peter raced for my friend and summer employer, Mac Williamson. Later, I schooled Pete over brush hurdles for his second career, way back in 1964.

your reply will be concise, and she will listen very nicely, then go out and do precisely what she wants."

But if you buy the wrong horse, and get burned, don't say I didn't warn you.

Thoroughbreds as Trail Horses/Distance Competitions

As people scramble to find second careers for the thousands of Thorough-breds that are coming to the end of their racing lives, one that may often be overlooked is trail riding and distance riding in its many varieties, including pleasure riding.

Bien Venue and Wintry Oak (see fig. 1.5) were two Thoroughbreds that I rode with success on the Green Mountain Horse Association (GMHA) 3-Day

1.5: Wintry Oak, a young, unraced Thoroughbred stallion placed second against mainly Arabians in the 1998 GMHA 100-Mile trail ride. Thoroughbreds are amazingly versatile athletes if we give them the chance to prove it.

100-Mile—a famous competitive trail ride in Vermont—and if they can do something as tough as that, they can do lots of things. But most Thorough-breds that survived flat racing will never again be asked to do anything as hard or as likely to cause injury as flat-out speed.

And discard the stereotype that OTTBs are usually hot. Some are, many are not. Not long ago, we went on a fairly long ride with a Morgan, a Warm-blood, and with Portada, a six-year-old mare by a son of Unbridled's Song who raced 16 times as a three- and four-year-old, and guess which one was the brave leader past the spooky stuff?

So add trail riding to the list. Thoroughbreds can be hugely versatile if you give them the chance to prove it.

The Warmblood

To even begin to comprehend the enormous diversity encapsulated in the word "Warmblood," we need to envision what it was like in Europe back in the early pre-World War II decades of the twentieth century.

As lifestyles based upon horses gradually became supplanted by lifestyles based upon the automobile, the truck and the tractor, horses began the slow slide toward obsolescence as the go-to options for work, transportation, and military usage.

The horse for sport and for hobby required less "ponderous" horses than those used for plowing fields and pulling wagons, so even prior to World War II, at the 1936 Berlin Olympics, for example, old newsreels show a lighter type of horse than what we would associate with transport and agriculture.

Then came about a decade of war, devastation, and destruction, and many thousands of horses died.

After the Second World War ended, by the late 1940s, as the various countries rebuilt, those involved with horse sport and horse breeding had to look down the road and begin to plan just what the horse of the future might need to be. The main European riding disciplines in the late 1940s were show jumping and dressage, with three-day eventing a distant third.

In order to lighten up and refine the heavier stock that were left over from pre-war agriculture, various countries began to experiment with crossing the heavy "cold-blooded" mares with "hot-blooded" Thoroughbreds and Arabians, in a sort of vast version of equine "mix'n'match," to produce "The Warmblood." The Selle Français was the French version, the Swedish Warmblood, Danish Warmblood, and Dutch Warmblood involved other breeding lines. In Germany, the breeds tended to follow geographic lines: Hanoverian, Holsteiner, Oldenburg, and so forth. The Trakehner remained close to its roots, but many of the breeds allowed superior horses from other breeds into the various studbooks.

To further complicate matters, much of this sport-horse breeding was specialized for either jumping or dressage, so that you might have two stallions that were Hanoverian, for example, but one would be from a jumping line quite distinct from the dressage lineage of the other.

In Ireland, local farmers crossed Irish Draught mares with Thoroughbreds and sometimes with Connemaras to create the Irish Sport Horse (see p. 37). "Warmblood" can mean many things to many people.

1.6: Partly forged in the terrible crucible of World War II, in terms of which horses survived, the mighty Holsteiner has come to be a dominant sport horse breed in the twenty-first century. This was Vianus, a Holsteiner I had at a Walter Christensen clinic in 1984.

The Holsteiner

In the fall of 1982, I spent a month riding at Stal Tasdorf. This stable was run by Walter Christensen, German dressage master and coach of the Swedish Olympic Dressage Team, located in the tiny, picture-postcard village of Tasdorf, near Neumünster, in the Schleswig-Holstein region of northern Germany. Most of the horses there were Holsteiners, and it was my first chance to ride a number of these powerful Warmbloods (fig. 1.6). Some of them were massive, others more refined, and I can remember Walter's explanation for the varying characteristics within the breed as deriving from "the invention of the horse trailer."

Before horse trailers, Walter explained, a breeder basically had to breed his mare to a stallion within horse-walking distance of the stallion, so regional differences were quite distinct. But after World War II, as the highways got repaired and the country struggled back on its feet, the breeding industry became more oriented toward the "modern" or "sport type," a lighter Holsteiner with more resemblance to the Thoroughbreds like Marlon and Ladykiller, stallions from England or Ireland, being used for breed refinement. This worried Walter, I remember. He said that if some "heavy" stallions were not bred to similarly "heavy" mares, to get young "heavy" fillies, the breed would gradually lose what Walter called "its seed corn."

> Although a horse may have greater or lesser innate talent for something, most horses are more versatile than many of us give them credit for.
>
> ■ ■ ■

The modern Holsteiner is not only *the* dominant force in modern Grand Prix show jumping, it's the Warmblood breed that is increasingly showing up in the pedigrees of modern event horses: Mark Todd's 2011 Badminton winner, Land Vision, has two crosses to the Holsteiner foundation sire Landgraf. Heinrich Romeike's 2008 Olympic gold-medal winner, Marius, is a Holsteiner. Mary King's Fernhill Urco is part Holsteiner, as is Buck Davidson's Ballynoe Castle RM. One of the leading eventing sires in Ireland, Cavalier Royale, was a full Holsteiner, and so it goes.

Many of the "young and future" event horses in the United States Eventing Assocation (USEA) classes are at least half Holsteiner, and as more of them win, my assumption is that more of them will be bred for eventing. The crosses that I've seen remind me of bigger, stronger Thoroughbreds, and many have that famous Holsteiner "big jump." They can move, and are surprisingly fast on cross-country, and that old "Dumblood" label that eventers once used to scornfully dismiss them is being replaced with growing respect and the acknowledgment that Holsteiners and Holsteiner-crosses can get it done at eventing's highest levels.

Beaulieu's Cool Concorde—One of My Current Warmbloods

Although "Cordi," a cross of several Warmblood breeds, was specifically bred to be a show jumper, I have always believed that a horse doesn't know what he's supposed to be, and although a horse may have greater or lesser innate talent for something, most horses are more versatile than many of us give them credit for.

I have done show jumping, distance riding, and dressage with Cordi. She is one of those no-drama horses that "lets" you ride her, and although Cordi can see a monster behind a bush in the deep forest, she basically goes along doing whatever job I happen to be asking her.

I think that much modern riding is increasingly specialized. Many ring riders won't go out of the arena. Many outdoor riders won't set hoof in a ring. Those who are not so limited are apt to have broader ranges of skills, more "arrows in their quivers." Cordi keeps me plucking back over my shoulder for new arrows…better than being stuck in a rut.

The Quarter Horse

Ask the average American about Quarter Horses, and if they know anything at all, it's likely they know the Quarter Horse is a "Western" horse, ridden generally by cowboys. It's a huge breed, with five million registered horses, probably more than most or maybe all the other breeds combined. And while it's true that the Quarter Horse was developed in the West as a horse suited to work cattle, it's equally true that thousands of Quarter Horses are ridden "English," in eventing, dressage, hunter/jumper, trail, endurance—anywhere that needs a "Steady Eddie" type of horse that's basically nonthreatening to the average rider (fig. 1.7).

Ask the average riding clinician which breed, including crossbreds, she sees most frequently in all sections of North America, and I'd be very surprised if the Quarter Horse weren't numerically at the top of the list. I've taught eventing clinics where half the horses were Quarter Horse types, prob-

1.7: One of my sons, Rett Emerson, on his Quarter Horse at a rodeo. Bred to be stock horses, originally, Quarter Horses have become the number one American breed in popularity and the largest breed registry in the United States—and the world. They are immensely versatile and willing partners, sane and reliable. We see them everywhere there are horses being ridden.

ably in part because they are so readily available, but also because they tend to come with a sanity button.

The term "hot Quarter Horse" is about as much of an oxymoron as "fast Percheron." There are some nervous, difficult Quarter Horses, inevitable in a population so huge, but that's not the norm. What's more normal is the kind, steady, confidence-building sort of horse that tolerates some rider mistakes without getting "bent out of shape," allowing the rider to develop skills that she might never discover on a horse that makes her tighten with nervous apprehension.

The average Quarter Horse ranges in height from about 14.2 to about 16 hands. Appendix Quarter Horses—so named because with a mixture of Thoroughbred blood, they are in an "appendix" to the main registry—can be taller, often depending on how much Thoroughbred has been added to the genetic mix. As their ranch and roping ancestry might predict, they tend to be somewhat stocky horses and not to have a high head carriage. How would *you* like to throw a rope off a horse that has his head up in your face? This lower head carriage can be something of a hindrance to jumping, where a "hocks-under, head-up" profile can make things go more smoothly, but many Quarter Horse riders are happy to forego some of the Thoroughbred and Warmblood physical traits if they can be assured of the perhaps steadier, calmer emotional traits that the Quarter Horse seems to be endowed with.

There's a wonderful saying that we would all do well to remember, "A horse doesn't know what he's supposed to be."

■ ■ ■

Some Quarter Horses, especially the massively muscled types bred for conformation classes, known as "halter classes," have bodies too big for their hooves, leading to a predisposition to navicular disease, and other limb problems. Another problem to be aware of is the disease known as HYPP, associated with the stallion Impressive. But these are avoidable, I think, with good pre-purchase awareness.

We may not associate the Quarter Horse with the upper echelons of some of the English riding sports. Badminton, Kentucky, and Wellington probably will remain the domain of other breeds and other types, but many of our upper-echelon riders got their start on Quarter Horses, just as thousands of American riders climb on Quarter Horses every day, knowing they have a gentle, sympathetic, and accommodating partner.

Heinz 57s (UNKs)

There are hundreds of horse and pony breeds that I either don't know anything about, or as the saying goes, "Know just enough to be dangerous." I know a little about Trakehners, Dutch Warmbloods, Hanoverians, Selle Français, Friesians, Hackneys, Paints, Oldenburgs, Appaloosas, American Saddlebreds, Standardbreds, and a few others, but not enough to be so rash as to try to come across as knowledgeable.

Each breed has its own breeders, riders, drivers, fan club, and support network, and it might be better to consult true breed experts, not Denny Emerson.

However, like most of us who've been in the horse world for a long time, I've been involved with hundreds of horses, probably thousands, that didn't come with any label attached (fig. 1.8). Some of them were probably registered, but the papers had been lost. Others might have been eligible for registry, but the paperwork was never finalized. The majority, though,

1.8: All I knew about Cat's breeding was the old saying, "by Cattle Truck out of Oklahoma." There are so many "UNKs" out there, "UNK" standing for breeding unknown. Some of the greatest athletes of all time have been "UNKs."

of these "breeding unknown" animals were probably a mix of one, two, or several breeds. There's a story about a little boy with his dog. Someone asked him what kind of dog it was. The little boy replied, "He's part Husky, part Collie, part Beagle, part Golden Retriever, part German Shepherd, and the rest is a mixture."

Cat

Cat was as plain and backyard as horses get when I bought him for $800 in the late sixties.

He'd supposedly been a barrel racer in Oklahoma, and he was scared of quick movements. I once saluted in a dressage test the way men did back then by removing my hunt cap and dropping my arm with the hat, and he spun, so there I was saluting not the judge, at letter C, but nobody, at letter E.

But here are some of the many lessons I learned from having to persevere with a less than "elite" horse because he was the horse I had, and the only horse I had.

The first lesson is that if you ride the same horse, day after day, week after week, month after month, year after year, you and that horse are going to know each other so well that despite the fact that you both have failings and insufficiencies, you

trust each other well enough to begin to create something bigger and better than either one of you alone.

Next is that most of us tend to "bail out" on a horse that is hard to ride, and one that does not win easily, but if you do not bail out, the talents that may be deeply hidden within both of you may have a chance of being discovered.

On Cat I did my first long-format Advanced event, at Dunham, Quebec, in 1971.

On Cat I jumped six feet in a knock-down-and-out jump-off at a Vermont summer jumper show.

I was able to do things on Cat that made it possible, a few years later, to be on a gold medal USET team at the Burghley, England, World Three-Day Event Championships in 1974, riding Victor Dakin.

I could not have done that on Cat. We were not good enough. But I would not have been able to do that *without* Cat, and the places in my riding that he allowed

So often, as time passes, and grade horses get bred to grade horses, back and forth and back and forth, these total mixtures begin to be the result, and while many of them are "just horses," every once in a while, a superstar emerges in defiance of all the hype and publicity surrounding the concept of "bred in the purple."

me to go. He made me ready for when the chance came.

In Retrospect: What I'd Do Differently with Cat

When you get a horse with an unknown background, you have to be something of a Sherlock Holmes to figure out, by what you see in the horse, what he has previously experienced and what you may need to do to help him recover from that, if he has been traumatized in any way.

Fifty years ago, with Cat, the "barrel racer from Oklahoma," I simply lacked the insight to know how to help him get over his sometimes almost panicked behavior.

If I had him today, my approach would be to do everything in my power to earn his trust. I would do groundwork, I would do lots of walking under saddle. I would try to get him to stretch, to gently bend, to get him over the idea that a human was an adversary—something

Cat was not my "ultimate" horse. But Cat gave me tactics and skills to use so that when Victor Dakin and York came along, I was ready and able to ride them. Sometimes the "stepping stone" horse is the one you cannot do without.

like the "lion at the water hole" that wanted to cause him pain.

Cat was typical of so many horses that are scarred from their interactions with humans. Some can be healed more successfully than others, but in all cases, patient, gentle handling is the way forward.

I was too inexperienced to know enough about that to help Cat recover.

Snowman was in a kill pen at New Holland. Nautical, Hugh Wiley's "Horse with the Flying Tail" (made famous by Disney) was by Cattle Truck x The West. My first pony, Paint, was one of these, my second horse, Bonfire, ditto. My gold medal horse, Victor Dakin, was supposedly part Thoroughbred, part "Irish," part Morgan, and part Arabian. (I've always been tempted to add, "and the rest was a mixture.")

There's a wonderful saying that we would all do well to remember, "A horse doesn't know what he's supposed to be." Sure, that's true within limits, but let's be real. A Percheron isn't going to win a race unless, maybe, it's a short race to the grain bin, and a Quarter Horse/Appaloosa cross is unlikely to clean Valegro's clock in Grand Prix dressage, but horses are amazingly versatile if we give them the chance to be, and don't let human preconceptions limit what we ask them to try.

Most of the great horsemen I've been around look first at the horse, then at the papers, except in the rarified world of racing, where pedigree can mean the difference, literally, between $5,000 and $500,000.

Total breed "fanatics" remind me of sports fans. They love (pick one: Morgans, Paints, Thoroughbreds, Holsteiners, whatevers) the same way people, old and young, love various professional sports teams. And once that obsession has been implanted, the most likely and effective cure is death!

All my life I've been lucky enough to be infatuated with lots of breeds, not just one, among which Morgans, Thoroughbreds, Irish crosses, Arabians, and various Warmblood crosses are the ones I've most closely dealt with, but I never knew York's breeding, and he was as good as anything I've ever sat on. As far as I'm concerned, a good mutt is a good horse.

I know that my son Jamie will never outgrow his obsession with the Boston Red Sox, nor my son Rett his love of the Boston Celtics. My dad spent most of his life worshipping at the altar of Dartmouth College football, so I can understand that blind devotion. But if I could give some advice to young horse lovers, I'd say try not to be that way with horses. Find a college, find a sports team, find a rock band, whatever floats your boat, to be your obsession, but try to look at the horse in front of you for what it is, not for the label attached.

Traditional Draft Crosses

Many years ago, in Europe, as farmers began to selectively breed big, strong horses to clear their woodlands, pull out stumps, plow, harrow, and mow their emerging fields, haul produce to market and basically become the tractors, bulldozers, and trucks of an earlier time, the various breeds that we collectively call "draft" horses began to take their varying forms. In due course, these horses found their way to North America.

If there is one character trait that a draft horse cannot have, it's "hot." I've watched local farmer Eddie Nelson, working in his woodlot in Vershire, Vermont, with his Belgian "Admiral." Eddie would let Admiral stand, fully harnessed, but untied, while he dropped a pine or hemlock. As the tree crashed to the ground, Admiral might twitch an ear. Or not.

Eddie would limb the tree with a snarling chainsaw, cut it into log lengths, go fetch Admiral and back him to the butt end of the log, where, again not tied in any way, Admiral would stand calmly while Eddie wrapped a pull chain around the tree, attached the other end to Admiral's tugs, picked up the reins, and clucked to his horse. As Admiral walked to the landing, Eddie would hop up on the dragging log to get a free ride.

Fast-forward to a North American three-day event. There will be a certain number of riders who may need a horse with a bit more size, perhaps a quiet temperament and a steady demeanor, but who might not be able to afford an Irish Draught cross, or a European Warmblood. Lo and behold, there's a Percheron half-bred gelding. Or a ¾ Thoroughbred, ¼ Belgian mare; or a ⅞ Thoroughbred, ⅛ Clydesdale. The top American horse on the gold-medal winning World Equestrian Games USET squad in 2002, John Williams' Carrick, was part Clydesdale, a 16th, I think. He was individually fourth in those Games.

Bold Minstrel

Bold Minstrel.

Bold Minstrel was a horse that has been described as the greatest American sport horse of the twentieth century. His owner, Bill Haggard, rode him to hunter championships, and later switched his focus to eventing. When Mike Plumb's Olympic horse Markham panicked and had to be put down on the plane to Tokyo, Bill Haggard flew Bold Minstrel to Japan as Plumb's replacement mount, and together they helped win the team silver medal in 1964.

There is irony in the story about Bold Minstrel in that he might never have been born. It used to be the practice of Thoroughbred breeding farms to have a few nurse mares available, usually some type of draft cross, in case one of the Thoroughbred mares died or was incapable of feeding her newborn foal. Bold Minstrel's granddam, a full or part Percheron, was just such a mare. She had been bred to a Thoroughbred stallion and subsequently delivered a filly destined to become the dam of Bold Minstrel. Had there been an orphan Thoroughbred foal born on the farm, it was then the unfortunate policy to put down the nurse mare's own foal.

Bold Minstrel's dam, Wallise Simpson, by Royal Minstrel, was spared that fate and grew up to be bred to another Thoroughbred stallion, Bold and Bad, to produce the part-bred foal, Bold Minstrel.

These solid citizen draft horses, like the Quarter Horses, and Quarter Horse crossbreds, come with a sanity button—installed by decades of selective breeding—to allow their farmer owners to work the land without having to deal with temperament issues. Many eventers are called "adult amateurs," meaning they have jobs, families, or other obligations that prevent them from the "all-day, every-day" riding that allows professionals to develop the expertise to deal with horses that come equipped with high-octane, eight-cylinder engines.

Draft breeds that aren't mixed with something else, usually Thoroughbred, tend to be too heavy and massive, often up to a ton, to make good riding horses. Some crosses, as they get "nearer the blood," as Jack Le Goff (in his heavily French accent) used to say about Thoroughbreds, will bring many of the same benefits as the wildly popular Irish Draught crosses. The American draft crosses, though, will lack the same "curb appeal" of the Irish Draught cross.

Irish Crossbreds

Admittedly, there are Irish Crossbreds, foaled in Ireland, that don't have a drop of "Registered Irish Draught" (RID), and are touted as "Irish Sport Horses." For example, there are lots of Thoroughbred mares in Ireland with essentially American pedigrees. Let's say one of these is bred to the Irish Sport Horse Cavalier Royale, who is a German-bred full Holsteiner. The resulting foal could be considered an Irish Sport Horse, but it wouldn't be what most breeders and riders think of when they think "Irish Cross."

The racing-bred Thoroughbred stallion crossed onto the RID or RID-cross mare is another classical manifestation. Thousands of international sport horses, especially in eventing, are mixtures of sleek racing machines crossed with strong, steady, calm, powerful Irish Draught (pronounced draft, as in draft beer) mares, the fillies crossed back again, and sometimes again and again, to create the horse that looks like a slightly bigger, stronger version of a Thor-

1.9: When I won a big Preliminary division at the Dauntsey Park Horse Trials in England, back in 1974 on Irish Warrior (donated to the USET by Patrick Butler), I was informed by one of the English girls, "Hey! You Yanks aren't allowed to come over here and beat us at our own events."

That fall, when the United States won the gold medal at the 1974 World Championships, half our winning team, Bruce Davidson's Irish Cap and Don Sachey's Plain Sailing, were Irish crosses as well. Fight fire with fire!

oughbred, with a bit more bone, a bit more uphill stature, and a bit steadier temperament (fig. 1.9).

Some people think that an Irish Sport Horse and an Irish Thoroughbred are basically similar, but if you study the pedigrees of the top stallions in Irish racing, you may be surprised at how many of them are either half or full American-bred Thoroughbreds. The leading Irish racing sire, Galileo, is by the

American-bred Sadlers Wells, son of Canadian-bred Northern Dancer. Galileo's dam, Urban Sea, descends from American stalwarts Mr. Prospector and Buckpasser.

The second leading sire, Montjeu, is by Sadlers Wells. Third place Distorted Humor, USA, is by a son of Mr. P. Fourth place stallion, Smart Strike, Canada, is by Mr. Prospector, and so it goes, air travel making the modern Thoroughbred a mixture of international breeding lines, whether in America, Ireland, or New Zealand.

How many crosses does it take to make a galloping sport horse out of "a plow horse that can hunt," which is how Ariel Grald describes the big solid mares that do farm work during the week, and then, on Saturday, follow the hounds through briars and bogs and thickets where we Americans wouldn't dare walk our dogs?

The first cross, the half-bred, might be a sturdy fellow (or mare). A heavyweight hunter to tote around a banker from Dublin who has gone to the country to hunt on the weekend.

The next cross toward refinement is a ¾ bred (¾ Thoroughbred, ¼ Draught) and depending upon its type might be a Preliminary Level eventer, or even an Advanced eventer, like David O'Connor's Giltedge or Custom Made. Bruce Davidson's Badminton winner, Eagle Lion, was ⅝ Thoroughbred, ⅜ Draught. Some are ⅞ bred, some ¹⁵⁄₁₆, by which point they are virtually big Thoroughbreds.

Karen McCollom, a Vermont event rider, rode her Irish half or three-quarter bred Inniscara around three Kentucky long-format three-day events, and two Checkmates, and would often be one of a handful to get the time on steeplechase. She describes the ideal cross this way, "Highly rideable and sensible, great jumpers, good movers, brave and hardy." It's as if they are foaled with a cross-country "go button" already genetically installed.

It may be that as Irish breeders bring in more Warmbloods from mainland Europe, the traditional Thoroughbred/RID cross will begin to be blended with other lines. To some extent, that's already happening, but there are still plenty of riders who believe in the traditional formula, and will resist being nudged away from a breeding formula that they consider totally tried and true.

The Arabian

Like many of us, I got my early impressions of the Arabian from reading all the *Black Stallion* books by Walter Farley, so that I erroneously pictured them as 17-hand giants. Then, in about 1954, when I joined a local 4-H Club, our

Loftus Fox

I was 60 when I bought Loftus Fox in Ireland, and my goal was to compete for 50 consecutive years in eventing at the Preliminary level or higher. Lofty would help me reach that goal.

The year I would turn 60 (2001) was my fortieth consecutive season of competing in three-day events at the Preliminary Level or higher. I've always been a goal-setter, and for some reason, I decided that a possibly attainable goal would be to continue to compete at Preliminary or higher for 10 more seasons, until 2011, when I would both reach 70 and have an uninterrupted string of 50 seasons.

That would be a hard goal, because it would mean that I had to stay brave enough to do it, healthy enough to do it, and motivated enough to do it, and I would need a horse that would let me do it.

club leader, Harold Manners, raised Arabs in Shelburne Falls, Massachusetts, and I got to see the real thing. What I remember most vividly from those visits was a blind broodmare who would locate her foal because Harold had a bell hanging around the foal's neck that the dam could hear.

Through my early Western and Morgan and 100-mile-trail-ride years, I don't remember riding an Arabian, although I admired them from afar, and it wasn't until sometime in the 1970s that I rode various Arabs in eventing clinics. I wouldn't say that Arabians are very common in eventing, partly because

I went horse shopping in Ireland with some clients in July, a month before my birthday on August 20, and I decided to buy a big, plain, bay, five-year-old gelding named Loftus Fox, in hopes that he would carry me through the next 10 years as I plugged along toward my goal.

By now, finally, I felt as though I was a decent trainer. One of life's many little unfairnesses is, "So soon old, so late smart," but if you let all of that stop you, you won't even start.

I'd ridden Irish horses before, but Lofty was my first true experience with that golden cross of Thoroughbred mixed with Irish Draught, and I began to appreciate why so many riders have ridden them to so much success.

Lofty was straightforward. There was never any drama. Whether that was his personal contribution, or a result of being part Draught, or partly a result of my better and quieter training methods, the fact was that whatever I asked, Lofty calmly did.

By the time I had reached my mid-60s, I realized that I was sort of the Lone Ranger of my age group, and that most of my contemporaries who I'd competed with for decades had hung up their helmets, or spurs, or boots, or whatever it is that you hang up when you hang it up.

But I never felt threatened by the risks of Preliminary, even as age 70 loomed, because Lofty was so quietly competent. He was good in dressage, and he was bold on cross-country, not some sort of whacko crazy brave, but brave because he was only asked to perform within his limits.

they are too smart and "self-preservationist" to blindly leap into the unknown. Someone described her first ride on an Arab, down a straight dirt road, as "pole bending without the poles," as the little monster shied from right to left at every imagined danger. Steve Rojek, an internationally famous endurance rider and long-time Arabian rider, breeder, and trainer, describes the Arabian as, "the only breed which, when you sit in the middle, both ends go up!"

In 1997, Lana Wright, the first woman to ride in the Olympics in three-day eventing in 1964 (and later turned endurance rider), invited me to ride Zion, a 14.1-hand gray Arabian, in a 100-mile endurance race in the Carolinas. Not having a clue what I was in for, I blithely said, "Sure, why not?" At midnight, in cold, pouring rain, every known (and a few unknown) body part screaming in agony, I finished my first one-day, 100-mile race. So, naturally, I wanted to buy an Arabian and do more endurance racing—sane, rational thinking never having been one of my strengths.

Since then, I've owned four Arabs, and ridden many more, and for sheer toughness and true grit, and efficiency of travel, nothing else I've ridden has come close (fig. 1.10). I've ridden Arabians in 2,300 miles of endurance rac-

1.10: "Ms Kharata Monet," shown here crossing the Ottauquechee River on the GMHA 100-Mile trail ride, was an Arabian mare that I'd bought in California. She'd previously completed the Tevis Cup race with a former owner-rider. Arabians came from war horse stock, far back, and are the main breed of choice for distance riding.

ing, finished seven one-day, 100-mile races, and in 2004 at age 63, I fulfilled one of those "bucket-list" dreams by finishing the Tevis Cup on Rett Butler, an Arabian great-grandson of Bask that I bought from Tammy Robinson in Saugus, California.

The Arabian breed, like the Morgan, the American Saddlebred, and a few others, has been basically split between show usage and sport usage, and those two worlds don't have much in common. The "park" riders want high knee action, and they often use heavy shoes and long shank bits to create what they call "animation." However, the Arabians I admire most are the ones who will give you their heart and soul, mile after mile, in the cold Carolina rain or on high canyon walls under a blazing California moon.

Arabian blood from centuries ago runs in the veins of most modern horses. What greater gift could we want?

> The Arabians I admire more are the ones who will give you their heart and soul, mile after mile, in the cold Carolina rain or on high canyon walls under a blazing California moon.
>
> ■ ■ ■

The Morgan

Over the years, various people have asked me, "What's your favorite breed?" no doubt expecting me to say Thoroughbreds or Irish Crosses or something pertaining to eventing. Rationally, I'm a Thoroughbred fan. I've ridden hundreds of them, competed them for 50 years, stood numerous Thoroughbred stallions, been a follower of racing, and know something about Thoroughbred pedigrees.

But you know that old saying about never forgetting your first love…

In 1950, when I was nine, my family moved to Greenfield, Massachusetts, which happened to be 23 miles from Northampton. My grandmother lived in Northampton, as did my Uncle John, and his sister, Aunt Miriam. They were convenient places to stay when I discovered the primary allure of that small, western Massachusetts town—it was the site of the National Morgan Horse

Show. Starting in 1952, I'd get dropped off at the Three County Fairgrounds on the first day of the show, usually with Jack Baker or some other friend, and get picked up several days later when the show ended.

For those days, we'd wander up and down the lines and lines of stalls, checking out the horses, hoping some of the riders would talk to us. We'd browse the tack shops, and from dawn until after dark, we'd sit in the covered bleachers, entranced by the action, whether as exciting as the half-mile race in harness, or as static as the model two-year-old stallions, it was all the same to us: totally intoxicating. Only horse-crazy kids, current or former, know that feeling.

Some of the famous Morgans of that era were Upwey Ben Don, Waseeka's Nocturne, Parade, Black Sambo, US Menmar, Ulendon, Cornwallis, Orland Vigildon, Orland Leader, US Panez, Bay State Wardissa, and Townshend Panabell.

The farm names, as vivid today as then: Windcrest, Green Mountain Stock Farm, Waseeka, Townshend, Broadwall, Orland, High Pastures, Bar-T, Ashland, Green Meads. The breeders, owners, riders: Johnny Lydon, Dr. Bob Orcutt, Nancy Ela, Anna Ela, J. Cecil Ferguson, Lyman Orcutt, Robert Lippitt Knight, Ted Davis, Susie Robinson, Jeannine Krause, Art Titus, Steve Tompkins, Kenneth Knapp, Stanley Crafts, Lawson Glidden, and on and on.

A few years later, in 1956, when I rode a grade Quarter Horse in my first GMHA 100-Mile, I rode with lots of Morgan owners, further fueling the Morgan flame. Later that fall, I (my parents, to be accurate) bought Lippitt Sandy as my first Morgan. I showed him at the National in Northampton in 1957, '58, and '59, and did the GMHA 100 in '57 and '58. Then, in '59, I worked for Robert Lippitt Knight, owner of the Green Mountain Stock Farm in Randolph, Vermont. This was before my freshman year at Dartmouth, and I rode Lippitt Rebecca for Mr. Knight in the '59 GMHA 100-Mile. The next two summers, I worked for the "Lippitt Farm," as most people thought of it.

Some other Morgans I rode, in addition to the ones I rode regularly at the Green Mountain Stock Farm, were Lippitt Raymond, my first stallion, who

I stood for $50; Lippitt Tweedle Dee, who I showed for Deane Davis (later to become governor of Vermont); and Miller's Commander, my father's driving horse, who I rode in the 1962 GMHA 100-Mile (see sidebar).

Then, in 1961, my friend Allen Leslie (later to become a well-known equine veterinarian) and I drove down to South Hamilton, Massachusetts, to watch the Wofford Cup, my first time seeing a three-day event. I got hooked, and for the next 50 years, didn't own a Morgan. But it was only on a (long) temporary hold, and in 2011, I bought High Brook Rockstar, a five-year-old Morgan

The Morgan: Millers Commander

This is a Morgan, Millers Commander, in South Reading, Vermont, on Christmas Day, 1960.

Robert Frost wrote about Morgans in several poems, including "The Runaway" and "Stopping by Woods on a Snowy Evening." I saw Robert Frost looking in at me over my stall door at GMHA as I was rubbing my Morgan's legs at the end of a 40-mile day. That was in 1957. I have always thought of Morgans since as stepping out of a Frost poem.

mare, from breeder and tack shop owner Laura Spittle in South Woodstock, Vermont. Roxie's pedigree includes Lippitt Sandy's full sister, Miller's Commander's dam, and Lippitt Raymond's and Lippitt Rebecca's sire, so it's old home week for me.

High Brook Rockstar

If my main goal was to do as well as possible in some distance-riding sport like competitive trail riding or endurance racing, I would "put the square peg in the square hole," and buy an Arabian, instead of riding a Morgan like Roxie.

But my goal is to promote the Morgan breed as a versatile breed that can do many different things well, and I have ridden Roxie in dressage shows, Morgan shows, competitive trail rides, and in one endurance race.

I grew up with Morgans, and although I spent 50 years in eventing, which is not a sport custom-made for the Morgan, I never lost interest in them. In fact, way back in Roxie's pedigree, a many time great-grandmother is a mare named Lippitt Sandra, by Lippitt Sam out of Bethal. Lippitt Sandra was a full sister of my first Morgan, Lippitt Sandy.

So when I am riding Roxie, I am, in a way, recreating my own riding past, and I find that to be far more satisfying than simply trying to win another blue ribbon—not that I don't like winning blue ribbons.

The Connemara

If ever there was a sport pony or small horse identified with eventing, it would be that quintessentially Irish breed, the Connemara, named after the Connemara region of County Galway, in the west of Ireland (fig. 1.11). There are all kinds of legends about the origin of these tough, hardy athletes, so pick one. Who's going to prove you wrong?

1. The Vikings brought their ancestors to Ireland.

2. They descend from the extinct breed known as Irish Hobby.

1.11: I rode this Connemara when I was judging some classes at the Royal Dublin Horse Show in Ireland in 2016. Connemaras and Connemara crosses are tough, brave, athletic, sturdy, and sound of mind and body. They are my personal favorite of the pony breeds.

3. When Spanish galleons from the Armada ran aground in 1588, Andalusians got loose and interbred with the native stock.

There's also Arabian, Thoroughbred, and Hackney blood in there, or so they say. Who cares? The Connemaras I know are little jumping and cross-country machines, sort of the pony answer to the Thoroughbred/Registered Irish Draught crosses that kick butt wherever eventers duke it out. The typical Connemara is an interesting mix of stocky and breedy, strong loins, crested neck, attractive head, strong hooves and limbs—an all-around athlete in a small package.

In the undiluted pony form, the Connemara is a great kid's mount, but plenty of small adults crave them, too. Crossed with the Thoroughbred, the sky seems to be the limit. I had a stallion, Forfeit, whose dam Fru (an international show jumper) was said to be part Connemara, and her full brother Foster was an individual bronze medal winner in the 1968 Olympics. Another of my advanced eventers, For Pete's Sake, was supposedly out of an unregistered Connemara mare. He could jump as well as any horse I've ever ridden.

> If I could get in one of those time machines and go back to being 10 again, I'd ride a Connemara.
>
> ■ ■ ■

Since I've personally had a couple of Advanced Level eventers that were part Connemara, I'd have to say that's my pony breed of choice. They're tough, they're good jumpers, and they can gallop. They outcross well, and they tend to be sound. If I could get in one of those time machines and go back to being 10 again, that's what I'd ride.

Abby Emerson, my granddaughter, riding Chai, a Connemara-Quarter Horse cross.

FDA Notice

The FDA has just reclassified the pony as a gateway drug.

The following is an actual, verbatim quote from an 84-year-old mother to her 61-year-old daughter, "Your father and I are waiting for you to outgrow this 'horse thing.'"

(The two statements above sum up about all that needs to be said on this subject....)

1.12: Many a small child has had her riding start on a small Welsh pony, one of the most beautiful breeds we can find. This is a dual trail and dressage pony, Whill's Kryptonite, a Section B, owned by Kathy Livingston.

The Welsh Pony—Small but Mighty

At the far end of the riding spectrum from the mighty draft horses are ponies, equines under 14.2 hands, and it's my guess that of the many breeds of riding ponies in America, Welsh Ponies and Welsh Cobs are among the most popular and most common. Cobs are basically "stockier," and ponies more refined, but that is a very broad generalization, and perhaps not very accurate (fig. 1.12).

I was a pony kid, too, but back in 1952, I had no idea of breeds or types, I just knew I wanted a pony. It was years later that I became aware of the various "sections" that define the different sizes and types of Welsh ponies.

According to my conversations and research, the Welsh ponies may have descended from the prehistoric Celtic Pony, and there were possibly Welsh

Ponies in Wales as early as 1600 BC. Because they had to endure the rugged conditions of a harsh climate, rocky terrain, and poor grazing, the breed that we know today became tough and hardy, basically through the survival of the fittest method of natural selection.

At some point, perhaps in the fifteenth century, some Arabian blood was added to the mix, but not so much that the breed characteristics were lost. Early Welsh Ponies did farm labor, hauled logs, pulled carts and buggies, and were used in coal mines. There is a theory that Justin Morgan, founder of the American breed of that name (see p. 43), may have been part Welsh, as early settlers to America brought these sturdy ponies to help settle the opening lands.

> One thing I know from lots of experience with ponies, and from Morgans and Arabians, is that small doesn't mean weak, incapable, or limited. It's the size of the heart that counts, and the size of the "try."
>
> ■ ■ ■

The modern Welsh registry was established in 1901 or 1902, and has been modified from time to time, but basically there are four "sections" of Welsh Ponies and Cobs, A, B, C, and D. For a full explanation, ask Mr. Google! Basically, Section A ponies are the little guys, under 12.2 hands. Section B ponies are over 12.2, but under 13.2 hands, and are slighter of build than Section C cob types, also under 13.2, but of stockier build. Section D Welsh Cobs are over 13.2 and don't have an upper size limit.

For all this complexity, there is one constant, which is that over the years, thousands of children have begun their riding careers on Welsh Ponies and Welsh Cobs. They've used them in Pony Clubs, they've followed hounds on them, they've jumped their first jumps, taken their first trail rides, and have had their first falls off Welsh Ponies.

I'm a pony fan for small kids and small adults. One thing I know from lots of experience with ponies, when I was a kid, and from Morgans and Arabians, when I was no longer a kid, is that small doesn't mean weak, incapable, or limited. It's the size of the heart that counts, and the size of the "try." Welsh Ponies are famous for having for lots of both.

Horse Shopping

There's a very old saying, "If you snooze, you lose," and I have found that over the years, if I wanted a horse that was for sale and I dithered and hemmed and hawed, I often lost the chance of getting the horse.

Which may not have been the worst conclusion, but my point is that if there is a horse for sale, and you think that you really want that horse, go try it, and not "next week" but right the heck now. And if you want him, pending vetting, try to hammer out a deal…right now.

I was recently on the selling end of one of these situations, and many people were disappointed, but those were people who did not jump fast enough.

In addition to the "snooze-lose" saying, there is another like it, "Strike while the iron is hot."

Consider the Older Horse

One of the biggest reasons so many green riders wind up with green horses that may scare them, or that at any rate prevent them from learning the way to apply correct aids, is because so many riders will not buy an older horse.

Consider Bold Minstrel at 16 (fig. 1.13). In his prime, at the height of his powers. Yet how many people do you know who would buy a 16-year-old horse?

They will say things like, "I want an investment." As if investing is only about money, and not an investment in learning how to ride, or in safety, or in the sense of security while learning that can come from an older, wiser, steadier horse.

So when I hear that cost is a prohibiting factor in finding a suitable horse that knows the deal and can help a green rider figure out "which buttons to push," I always suspect that those are riders who automatically carry some type of prejudice against "investing" in an older horse. The older, been there, done that horse is a great investment, but not so much in terms of

1.13: I know people who won't even think about buying an 11-year-old horse because "he's too old." At 14 here, Bold Minstrel's prime years were yet to come. A year later, he and Steinkraus cleared the puissance wall at Madison Square Garden set at 7 feet, 3 inches. Too old?

getting a later financial return as in investing in the process of giving the young or green rider the chance to learn correct basics that will last them all their riding years.

Most green riders who struggle with equally green horses are not learning correct basics. They are "investing" in the wrong piece of the riding puzzle.

Make That List Now to Help Avoid Heartache Later

There are thousands of horses and ponies out there, all over the world, and many of them are for sale. There are thousands of potential buyers. There are numerous methods of putting these horse buyers in contact with the horse sellers, the internet being the big game in town. There's also word of mouth, and there's print advertising, but whatever the method, at some point, some of the shoppers actually find themselves in the physical presence of some of the animals that are for sale.

There are two very broad, often overlapping methods of thinking that describe the horse-shopping experience, which I will call "Rational Thinking" and "Fairy Tale Thinking": RT and FTT. Most of us use both. Even the most hard-bitten, cynical, "been there, done that," curmudgeonly old pessimist will find something to hope for in the occasional horse. Even the most Black Beauty-ized, dream-struck, "I love his cute little ears" fantasizer doesn't fall in immediate love with every horse. But if you use a 1–to–10 scale on people, with 1 being the straight realist and the 10 the total dreamer, it might be a useful exercise to try to figure out where you might fit on this hypothetical scale.

Why? Because buying the right horse brings great satisfaction and joy, and buying the wrong one brings just as much dissatisfaction and distress, and even though choosing wisely can still lead to mistakes, choosing foolishly is more likely to turn out badly (fig. 1.14).

1.14: Beauty can cloud judgment. We go out to buy certain qualities, are smitten with physical splendor, and we come home with something other than our original objective. As it turned out, Epic Win, this Thoroughbred stallion, had beauty plus brains, soundness, and athletic ability. I was lucky!

If you know, deep in your heart, that you are an 8, 9, or 10, prone to gasp in delight at a glorious forelock, hiding two bright brown eyes, and overlooking the crooked left pastern, you might want to get a "3" friend to go with you. Even more important, sit down with that "3" friend, someone who knows you pretty well, and do the single best thing you can: write a list. That list can contain the "wishful" items I mentioned on page 15, and it should also pose some of the questions I mentioned at the beginning of this chapter.

One of the most important questions to struggle with before you get started on your list will also be the hardest question to face honestly: "How competent a rider and trainer am I?"

> **Make a list of the things in a new horse that you actually *need*, instead of the things that you *want*.**
>
> ■ ■ ■

Another hard question to answer honestly is: "What are my goals with this horse?"

If you fake the answers to these two questions, God help you, because nobody else can.

Example: You are at this point in your riding (which you refuse to face) an inexperienced rider who lacks stability, hasn't done much jumping, hasn't spent long hours hanging around barns and warm-up rings, so doesn't know much about horsemanship, and isn't very physically fit. Every one of these facts about you can be remedied, but they have not been addressed yet.

But you fantasize that you want a horse that can jump 3 feet 8 inches, and allow you to compete at the Preliminary Level of eventing. He must be a splendid mover, have a great gallop, and be beautiful and "electric" in dressage. Your goals are not in sync with your riding capabilities. Not yet.

And if you buy a horse that's too far above your capabilities who won't let you fumble around and make all kinds of mistakes while you gradually become a better rider, you may get scared or discouraged or injured, or all of the above, so that you may never become the rider that the right horse for you, at this time, might have allowed.

So make a list of the things in this new horse that you actually *need*, instead of the things that you *want*. Obviously, if you are multiple gold-medalist Michael Jung making the list, or some other great rider, the qualities you want are also those that you need, but that's not the case for most horse shoppers. So try to list those things that *you* need—in reality, for this particular stage of your riding—knowing that in a few years, or less, you may need something very different. Or not.

The Question Nobody Wants to Answer
Can you sell him if he's not Mr. Right?

This discussion about buying horses is about to become less comfortable. If you are, let's say, a golfer, you will have a set of golf clubs. A skier will have skis, a tennis player a tennis racquet. As new and improved clubs, skis, racquets are developed, the competitive athletes in these kinds of sports will probably upgrade to the equipment that will be more likely to give them that "edge" we all talk about.

In professional sports, players are constantly being traded or sold, as the managers and officials of the various teams are also constantly trying to upgrade. We are used to seeing headlines like: "Bosox Trade Miller for New Shortstop Lorenzen."

If emotion could be left out of the equation, the upwardly mobile riders would be continually attempting to get better strings of horses, and that's exactly what many of them do. There are horses being bought and sold across the competitive spectrum every day, across all sectors of the riding world, for all kinds of reasons. In many cases, a rider will sell one horse to make room for another that she believes is a better horse for the discipline in which she is trying to excel. Many of the top competitive riders think of horses, in a way, as items of sports equipment. This does not mean these people are callous or hard-hearted or don't love animals. It does mean that their goals and priorities are different from those who buy a horse "'til death do us part," like a kitten or a puppy.

Is one way "right" and the other way "wrong?" It depends on your goals and beliefs, I think. The competitive riders can't be competitive on the big stage unless they think like the general manager of the Red Sox. If the New York Yankees have a superior pitching staff, and if the Sox want to make the playoffs, the Sox had better buy or trade for some better pitching.

If the whole idea of selling Dobbin makes you cringe and cry, don't sell Dobbin. Accept the tradeoff, that you will have less success than with a better horse (mover-galloper-jumper-whatever), but the emotional price of the tradeoff is too high. It has to be the answer that is right for you.

This whole dilemma is a big reason that it's very important to think carefully about the breeding or buying ramifications *before* you breed or buy, especially if you're pretty sure you won't be emotionally capable of divesting yourself of the foal or purchase when things don't work out as hoped or planned. Because the question that nobody wants to answer, so very often, is this: "Why don't you sell that horse and get a better one?"

There's only one person who has the answer to this question, of course, and it's the person who is being asked the question.

Hesnogoodbutilovehimsoicantgetridofhim

If your mental machete is sharp enough to hack through the verbiage of this heading, you can probably also understand and maybe even empathize with the dilemma it implies. Most of us have found ourselves possessed of or possessed by the wrong horse. Wrong for any of a thousand valid and invalid reasons: too hot to ride, too unsound, too poor a mover, too limited over a fence, too unpleasant in the barn, too old, too young, too big, too small—too unsuitable for what we actually need to have.

Sometimes the unsuitability has come in the flash of an eye. He hobbles in from the field one morning with a non-life-threatening but athletic-career-ending injury. Or, as with incipient navicular disease, it has been sneaking up, month by month. Or we've had one too many spin-and-fall-off episodes.

Or too many refusals at too many events or shows. Whatever and however the cause or reason, deep down we know that this is not the horse that can take us to places we want to go.

Now what?

If the horse is a pet, and you don't care if you actually ride or not, and if the unsuitability only renders the horse unfit for riding, you can just keep on keeping on. Or if you are rich enough to turn him into a pasture ornament and still get one or more other horses that you can ride, you are also just fine. You aren't the person I'm addressing.

> Most of us have found ourselves possessed of or possessed by the wrong horse.

But what if you do love to ride, don't have extra cash under your mattress, can't successfully ride this one, but can't bear to part with him? This is a real dilemma that thousands of riders face every day and there's no easy, one-size-fits-all answer. In the case of long-term unsoundness, there's the euthanasia issue. In the "old days," when horses were utilitarian and there was little cash for luxuries, this was done all the time out of sheer economic necessity.

I know lots of people who basically look at the issue like this: This horse is lame. It's not a question of whether he will be put down, but when. If I can't give him away, and can't afford to keep him and another, then now is better than later since it's unavoidable anyway, and just a matter of when.

For those who aren't able to face this, I guess they just have to stop riding while they wait for the horse to get old enough to die.

There are plenty of sound horses, though, but wrong for other reasons, like some I mentioned. Just because a horse might be a bad jumper or not have a fancy enough trot to make it in dressage might not mean he can't make a nice trail or pleasure horse. The rider has to choose. "Do I want a horse that's a round peg that I'm trying to force into the square hole, or would he be happier in a more fitting job, and would I be happier with one that seems suited to my ambitions?"

There is one key in all of this. The right choice has to be your choice. You are not a bad person if you put down a lame horse now rather than four years from now, unless you think you are. You don't have to be well mounted, but you probably should be if your main aim is to get ahead in your riding.

So, look at the horse you have. Look at your real goals. Then decide a best course of action. Or not. (Since putting this off is what you've been doing anyway!)

Breeding Your Own?

Here are four phases of "selective breeding" that demonstrate what enormous changes have taken place within the last century.

In early years, the only way to breed your mare to a stallion of your choice was to either ride or drive your mare to the stallion, or to ride or drive the stallion to the mare.

I have seen old Morgan stallion ads from the late 1800s, early 1900s, that some stallion would be at, say, the Tunbridge General Store on June 3 and 4, 1887, and that you could breed your mare "for 50 cents the leap."

This gave breeders a rather strict local limit as to the quality available.

Then along came better roads and the horse trailer. Now, your choices broadened to include stallions within a several-hundred-mile radius, basically, out as far as you were willing to drive your mare.

Then came another huge breakthrough: live, cooled semen, shipped in the Equitainer, so that you could pick out a stallion far from the mare, as air travel shrank the continent.

And now, with frozen semen and the internet, a breeder in Topeka, Kansas, can visually shop the world, order frozen semen from somewhere in Europe, or anywhere else on earth, and breed the mare at home, if there is someone around who understands the techniques of frozen semen.

And as for that, we also now have the possibility of cloning, the implantation of frozen embryos, and surrogate dams—who can say what will come next?

2

Horse Management

Common Ground

I once asked a man who owned a dude ranch in Montana what he fed the dude string during those long, cold winters. He replied, "We feed 'em snow and scenery."

That is one end of the horse-management spectrum. At the other end is what we might call "hothouse flower" *over*management: horses rarely turned out and when they are, they're as covered with protective boots and bandages and blankets as the armor-covered horses that thirteenth-century knights rode into battle.

There is a saying, "Ask 10 horse people a question and you will get 15 different answers." But most horse people agree on a few management issues:

1. All horses need water they can get to readily, water that is not scummy and disgusting in some slime-filled pail half full of decomposing hay.

2. All horses need to eat. What they eat—whether it's grass, hay, hay cubes, grain, or supplements—will be a matter of argument, discussion, and disagreement.

3. Worming is one of the most normal safeguards against the big horse killer, colic. Most horse people have some sort of deworming protocol.

4. Hoof care, dental care: Some do, some don't. The more responsible horse owners do. What that care consists of ranges all over the map.

5. Shots against diseases are normal in many stables, but not in all.

6. Then there are those tack-related questions: what sort of bits to use, what saddles, saddle pads…. These may also be considered under the heading "Horse Training," but because misuse of these items of tack can cause pain and distress, I think they also fit under the heading of "Horse Management."

The Basic Decisions

Where should a horse live? Some horses live 24/7 in a stall in a barn. Others live outdoors 24/7. Many live in stalls for part of the day and out part of the day. How much of one versus how much of the other is best, is also an ongoing subject of debate.

Barn design, farm design, paddock and pasture design and layout, and types of fencing are another big subject. Horse transportation, vanning, trailering, and trailer design also fit under general "Horse Management."

Just consider the various human occupations that deal with managing the well-being of the modern horse, and you will get a hint of the complexity of the subject.

The veterinarian. But wait! What kind of veterinarian? Because there are any number of specialists under that broad heading, are there not? Some deal with general health, others specialize in lameness diagnostics, others with radiograph technology. Some do colic surgeries, others specialize in limb repair, some with issues of the eye, some with dental care. And there are veterinary technicians in supporting roles for all these specialties.

The issue of shoeing or not shoeing, types of shoes and protective boots, hot shoeing, cold shoeing, trimming—it continues. The farrier, like the veterinarian, is one of those "can't do without" specialists whose trucks we routinely see rolling down our farm driveway.

Then there are massage therapists, acupuncturists, and horse chiropractors.

Many show stables employ grooms to keep both barns and horses neat and clean.

> Consider the various human occupations that deal with managing the well-being of the modern horse, and you will get a hint of the complexity of the subject.
>
> ◼ ◼ ◼

There are also feed companies, pharmaceutical companies, online purveyors of tack and horse equipment, and the places that sell pitchforks, wheelbarrows, sweat scrapers, buckets, and farm equipment (fig. 2.1 A & B).

Horse management is brushing the sweat marks off your horse's back before you put the saddle on for your next ride.

Horse management is a multi-faceted, multi-billion dollar international industry.

Horse management is all that lies between these two ends of an enormous spectrum.

The more you know, generally speaking, the better the decisions you can make to help your horse live a comfortable existence.

Saddle Fit, Saddle Selection, and Saddle Cost

If you have ever been on a hike and got a blister, and been way out there with no recourse but to keep hiking, you will appreciate what it must be like for the horse in distress from a badly fitting saddle.

I read that during the Napoleonic Wars, the French cavalry could be

2.1 A: Grass in the summer, hay in the winter is the most basic forage. Here, Kendall Szumilas is loading hay into the Gator to haul around to feed the various paddocks.

smelled by the enemy forces from the stench of the wounds on the horses' backs. How disgusting is that?

Get a saddle that fits, and get a girth that doesn't rub, and get clean, soft, absorbent saddle pads, and make darn good and sure that your saddle isn't making your horse uncomfortable when you ride him.

Horses' backs come in all shapes and sizes, and there is no such thing as a "one size fits all" saddle, no matter how many saddle pads you use to concoct a fit.

It's easy to get suckered into thinking that saddle suitability and saddle price are closely linked, and sometimes an expensive custom saddle will make you and your horse feel as if you have gone to heaven, but there are thousands of saddles out there, and if you shop and shop you can find one within your budget that will make you smile.

2.1 B: Horse management involves human manual labor. Some do it themselves, some farm it out to others: Kendall with Nathan Merchant on a familiar "parade of the wheelbarrows."

The key is to not just settle for "sort of okay." If you don't really like how the saddle feels, or if the saddle seems not to be a good fit for your horse, keep looking. There are so many styles and varieties that somewhere the right one is waiting, but you will need to hunt. I think it's worth the search, though, if you can't spring for the custom-made saddle that costs more than a good used car.

I have taught clinics where I've sat in 10 or 15 saddles over the course of the clinic, and in some I felt as though I could ride, and in some I felt as awkward as a rank beginner. Saddle fit absolutely can help or hinder you, and not just a little bit, but a whole lot. Get the right saddle. If you take good care of it, and it doesn't get stolen, you can keep it for decades. So keep hunting until you get it right. But, just because it's right for you does not mean, as I said earlier, that it will be the right fit for the comfort of the horse.

What Does My Horse Need?

Need Number 1: Safety

Horse behavior experts generally agree that the three things that horses want most, in order of importance, are safety, food, and the companionship of other horses.

"Safe from what?" might be a logical question, and since his safety is your horse's most critical need and desire, let's think about what this might mean.

In a wild herd situation, which is the way the horse evolved as a species, safety probably means being safe from being killed or injured. Horses are herbivores, and as such are a prey species unlike carnivores such as wolves and mountain lions. So the safety from being attacked and eaten must be right up at the top of the list.

Horses also get attacked by other horses—mares by stallions, lower-pecking-order mares by higher-pecking-order mares, and stallions constantly by

2.2 A & B: An old Wyoming rancher told me years ago, "Remember, boy: These horses we ride today, they're the ones whose daddy didn't get eaten by the lion at the water hole. Being spooky is not always a bad thing." Atti spots the "terrifying" rock. I let her stand, she takes cautious steps forward, and finally sniffs the rock.

one another. It is a scary jungle out there for the wild horse, and fear is a dominant emotion.

Think about this: Fear is the opposite state of feeling safe. So now we have this prey species under the "care, custody, and control" of another species: human.

It now gets pretty simple. Do we act as just another set of predators, bringing fear and pain into the lives of our horses, or do we try to minimize that anxiety and discomfort through humane handling and considerate training?

Anything we do with a horse or to a horse either causes fear or does not. Anything we do with a horse either causes discomfort or pain, or does not. We can judge our interactions with horses quite simply by asking two questions: Am I scaring this horse? Am I hurting him? Your stature as a true horseman or horsewoman will be largely dependent upon those answers (figs. 2.2 A & B).

> We can judge our interactions with horses quite simply by asking two questions: Am I scaring this horse? Am I hurting him?
> ■ ■ ■

I don't think good horse people are unkind or rough, and they are certainly not brutal. They may cause the horse some degree of pain, like giving shots with needles or while administering other veterinary care, or while restraining a horse that might hurt himself or hurt humans, but the good horse person doesn't use routine roughness or think of a horse as an adversary to be subdued and mastered.

Good horse people are systematic about training. They don't use harsh restraints or bits that cause pain or saddles that pinch or rub the horse raw. They never whip and spur in fits of anger. They don't torture horses with leverage devices like tight bitting rigs or draw reins. They don't think of horses as "bad" and deserving of "being punished." They break up their training sessions with little rest breaks and they try to quit after mild progress, rather than grinding for "perfection." A horse feels relatively safe in the hands of a good horse person. A good horse person wants the horse to feel safe. How simple is that?

Need Number 2: Food

In Walt Disney films, happy herds of horses frolic in lush green pastures. They are shiny, sleek, and well fed. In real life, many wild horses struggle to find enough to eat. Many are riddled with worms. Many are thin from malnutrition.

The knowledgeable horse manager will intuitively understand that old adage, "The eye of the master maketh the horse fat." She will feed good clean hay, grain, and supplements as needed. She doesn't want the horse skinny and "ribby," but she isn't feeding stockyard cattle. She wants the horse to look like a well-fed athlete, neither scrawny nor porky. These days, most of the major grain companies have expert nutritionists on staff, and they are usually ready to answer any questions you have. Veterinarians can help, too, if you have problems. There isn't much excuse, short of serious illness, to have malnourished horses in the twenty-first century.

2.3: I've been told that a horse's three main needs are safety, food, and the companionship of other horses. If all three can be satisfied simultaneously, that's the best case scenario for the horse.

Need Number 3: The Company of Other Horses

Horses are herd animals, and most horses prefer to be with other horses or donkeys rather than live in solitary confinement. If you have a horse, try to make sure he has a friend (fig. 2.3). I won't belabor this point. You know what you need to do.

Overall Management

So let's say you have a horse whose three basic needs are mostly met. He isn't afraid, or at least isn't most of the time—horses being horses, they all have things they spook at and worry about. He is well fed. And he has at least one friend. Now what else?

York

Although Victor Dakin was the most famous of my dozens of good horses, it was a New Zealand-bred that I bought in 1976 through expatriate Lockie Richards (one of my early eventing coaches) who had the most innate talent for eventing. York could do it all. He was sound and fast and brave and he could move like a cat, and he could jump anything I pointed him at.

I use York to demonstrate that old adage that the satisfaction of achievement is in direct proportion to the struggle exerted in its fulfillment. For all of York's towering talent, he came with two towering liabilities, neither of which were his fault.

York had massive old healed scars on his hip. I was told that he had been shipped from New Zealand to compete in an event in Australia, and he was in a crate of some sort in the hold of a ship. Apparently the container slipped or tipped, or perhaps York just got scared at being so tightly confined and panicked, but whatever the reason, he got hurt pretty badly, and ever after, was hugely claustrophobic.

He would charge through narrow doors, and because of that, hit his hips,

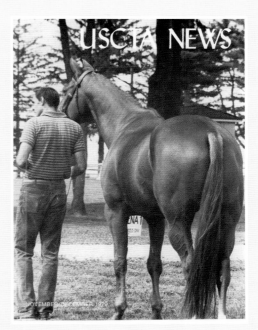

USCTA NEWS

NOVEMBER/DECEMBER 1976

Probably the most gifted athlete I ever rode, York, was dangerously claustrophobic because of an earlier accident, and he was a "victim" of insufficiently understood worming procedures from 40 years ago. He rose above all that to excel in American eventing in the heart of the long-format era.

and scare himself even more. In our big barn in Strafford, Vermont, the third stall door on the left is about three feet wider than the other stall doors. We built that for York 40 years ago so that he would be less afraid going in and out of his stall.

Trailering could be a nightmare. If he got scared, he would crowd the

(continued)

Many of us have visited show barns or breeding barns where the horses live in what most normal humans would think of as palatial estates. The brass fittings are gleaming. Polished halters and coiled lead shanks hang on each stall door. The flooring is cobblestone. Golden straw comes up to the knees and hocks of the royal inhabitants of the 14 by 14 foot stalls. Chandeliers hang overhead. The last cobweb got banished in 1947. Outside, there are mani-

York (continued)

wall, and if some person was in the way, too bad for the person. Over time, we learned how to avoid pushing his mental buttons, but that awful claustrophobia never went away.

About six months after York arrived in Strafford, during the summer of 1976, we noticed that he was losing weight. We upped his grain, but he continued to get thinner and thinner.

My friend Allen Leslie, who was one of the principles of the Delaware Equine Center, speculated that he might have cancer. We sent him down to Allen, and they opened him up the way they do for colic surgery. They discovered that his intestines were riddled with worms. Back in those days, horses were tube wormed twice a year, once in the fall and once in the spring, and York had been wormed, but it hadn't done the

job. Some of the veterinarians at the Delaware Equine Center, and some that they consulted at New Bolton, speculated that perhaps York, like others from Australia and New Zealand they had treated, had little resistance to the parasite populations in North America.

Recovering from this took York a long time. I used to just turn him loose on our lawn, which had the best grass, and he would graze and graze. We bought him big bags of carrots from a produce store because he could digest them more easily than hay, which was more coarse.

Gradually, gradually over months, the light began to return to York's eyes and he began to fill in over his gaunt ribs and hips, but it took almost two years before I could ride him again. But by 1978, when I did start competing him, I realized that I was sitting on a mega-ath-

cured grass paddocks. Fountains splash and play along the paths between the barns and the pastures. Banks of flowers adorn the walkways. The horses gleam like brand new copper pennies. Their hooves glisten from hoof oil, their bridle paths are trim, their manes are pulled, their tails are banged.

Over yonder, three miles down the pike, there is a big field with a three-sided shed at one end. Five dirty horses loaf in the shade of an overarching

lete who made hard things easy.

By the fall of 1979, when I took York down to Chesterland, the US National Advanced Three-Day Championships, York was fully back in action. He stormed around that big course as though it were some Pony Club test, and became the US Champion Event Horse.

Later that year, he also won the title of USEA Event Horse of the Year.

The horse who almost died, who teetered on the brink for two years, health restored, returned to world-class form. Never before or since have I been privileged to ride a horse that could do so much so easily.

In Retrospect: What I'd Do Differently with York

Apart from various riding strategies, one of the biggest "I wish I had known then what I know now" factors was the way that medical advances have dramatically improved over the years. I think that the cutting-edge technologies of 2018 in veterinary medicine have transformed our expectations of what is possible, especially with older horses.

Just as our worming strategies and what products we use for worming have changed, so have joint injections added years to the careers of countless horses. Stem cell therapies, advances in scanning and imaging, shoeing techniques—all these and more are making the modern horse of 15 years and older seem like the 1970s horse of eight or 10 years old.

These technologies were not readily available when I had York, so in a way it is inaccurate to use them as an example, but since he was a poster child for the need for better worming protocols, I cite them here.

tree. Their manes are long and scraggly. Their tails may even have some knots from burdocks.

But here's the thing. The horses in the show barn may be no more "happy" and no more content with their state than the five rough out horses, provided certain conditions have been met for both groups.

The first condition is that they are all well fed and have access to clean, fresh water.

Other conditions:

- All of them are on a deworming program.
- All of them have regular dental care.
- All of them have regular farrier care.
- All of them have routine veterinary care, such as vaccinations.
- All of them get checked daily for any injuries they might have picked up from running, getting kicked, or caught in the fence—those all-too-normal accidents.

All the rest is gloss, all the brass, the oiled halters, fittings, the flower beds, the light fixtures, the trimming, and hoof oil. It is calculated to impress other humans, because the horses could not care less.

In fact, the horses that are free to roam at will may well be more at ease than those trapped in the gilded cages of the show barns.

Keeping a Horse—In, Out, Some of Each?

Some horses live their entire lives in wide open spaces, their only shelter from wind, storm, rain, and snow a copse of trees, perhaps, or a dip between two hills. For wild horses, of course, this is their only reality, but many domesticated horses are kept outside, and are only brought into a barn to be tacked up, or shod, or dealt with medically.

Some horses live their entire lives in 10 by 10 foot boxes, the only time

Lippitt Sandy

The National Morgan Horse Show was held every July for about a week at the fairgrounds in Northampton, Massachusetts, 23 miles south of Greenfield. As I mentioned earlier, my grandmother and my Aunt Mim both lived in Northampton, so in 1953, just a month before my twelfth birthday, my father dropped me and my riding friend Jack Baker off at the show so we could watch the action for a few days.

I think that unless someone has direct contact with a particular breed or riding discipline, you are sort of "fair game" when it comes to having your interest snared by almost any breed or style of riding. It was that immersion in Morgans at "The National," coupled with seeing lots of Morgans at my first distance ride, the 1956 GMHA 100-Mile in Woodstock, Vermont, that made me into a Morgan convert.

I wanted a Morgan, and it turned out that a Mrs. Audrey Carter, from nearby Montague, had Lippitt Sandy for sale. In the fall of 1956, my parents bought Sandy for me.

In those days, people did everything with Morgans: rode them saddle seat, Western, and "balanced seat," drove them, raced them in harness, trail rode, and there was even a class at The

(continued)

When I got Lippitt Sandy just after my fifteenth birthday, and got to know Robert Lippitt Knight, Sandy's breeder, it triggered my interest in pedigrees that has continued through the 60 years since. Here, Sandy is completing the first day of the 1957 GMHA 100-Mile Competitive Trail Ride in Woodstock, Vermont.

Lippitt Sandy (continued)

National called the Justin Morgan Performance Class, which included pulling a stone boat as one of the phases. By 1957, when I showed Lippitt Sandy in Northampton, I had learned to drive and pull a stone boat so that I could enter that class, which also included a half-mile race in harness and a half-mile race under saddle.

That fall, I entered Sandy in my second GMHA 100-Mile Competitive Trail Ride, and received my second completion in that tough test.

Sandy, and that Morgan world, pointed me toward thinking that becoming a versatile horse person was normal. My experiences with several types of riding and training taught me something about my own particular way of learning. Instead of carefully learning how to do something *before* I did it on any sort of public stage, I would just plunge in, in sublime ignorance and optimism, and hope that I figured it out as I went along.

I'm not saying that is the right way for everyone, but it has been the right way for me, probably because I want to get on with whatever it is that grabs my interest. Others may be best served in other ways.

In Retrospect: What I'd Do Differently with Sandy

Back in 1956, and in many respects, to this day in 2018, Morgans tended to be shown and ridden with more hardware in their mouth than they ought to have. And while I think it doesn't hurt to know how to ride in a double or "full" bridle, with a snaffle and a long-shanked curb rein, I do think that the same horse would usually go more softly and comfortably in a simple snaffle.

Generally, and this is perhaps painting with too-broad brush strokes, there are two different methods of "riding the mouth." One is to think of the mouth of a horse as the source of the brake mechanism, so that a pull on the reins creates enough discomfort in the mouth that the horse slows down or stops. The other method is to think of the mouth as a delicate place and to try to preserve the trust of the horse in the rider's soft, feeling, "negotiating" hands.

When I was 15, 16, and 17, I didn't understand the nuances of soft hands, and I also used too much bit on Lippitt Sandy, and those are two situations I would go out of my way to change if I had the chance of a do-over with him.

they see the light of day being when they are ridden out of doors.

Between the total "outies" and the total "innies," there many variations:

One common method is to have the horse basically live in a stall, but have some daily turnout, either alone or with other horses in paddocks, ranging in size from as small as 20 by 20 feet, up to fields and pastures of several acres or more.

Another common method is the paddock or field with a run-in shed that allows the horse maximum freedom of movement while still providing free-choice shelter against the harsher elements. These sheds can be one-, two-, or three-sided, and sometimes horses use them when you think they should, and sometimes they don't.

> **Horses that are free to roam at will may well be more at ease than those trapped in the gilded cages of the show barns.**
>
> ◼ ◼ ◼

There is an old saying, "Damned if you do, damned if you don't," that applies to the choice that you make about how your horse should be maintained. If you keep him out in the healthy, fresh air, he can run and break a leg and die. If you keep him in a stall, he can get cast and break a leg and die.

What's the Right Approach?

If you ask five horse people the best way to keep a horse, you are apt to get six different answers. It is such an individual choice. My personal choice is to have paddocks or fields with sheds. This setup allows the horse to breathe fresh air, run around when he wants to run around, and still be able to stand under cover from cold rain or wind or blazing sun, or flies.

Of course, this method presumes that you have enough land, and many horse farms don't. For many stable owners, the stall and turnout option is the only option. It's a lot more work, this back and forth between barn and paddock, especially if it's also a matter of blankets on, blankets off, protective boots on, protective boots off. It's easy to see why so many horse owners who have the physical space just turn them loose and pray that they survive.

The thing that I would emphasize is that if your own horse is kept in a stall, you make the attempt to get him out as often as possible. Yes, horses have a high threshold of boredom, but sitting in a box stall 24 hours a day, day after day, month after month, just seems to me like serving a life sentence in jail. Ride him, turn him out, or do both, as best you can. That's my advice. We humans think horses love indoor shelter in bad weather, but most horses, given the choice, if their stall doors are open, and the barn door is open, will go right out into the storm. Their needs are not our needs.

3

Horse Training

Horses don't speak English. Or German. Or French. Nor do they speak any known human language. So, if we want to communicate with a horse, we need to figure out some sort of language that both of us can understand. We need to be able to "talk" to each other in some manner.

Lines of Communication

Imagine you are sitting at a table in a restaurant and a man sitting at a nearby table says, "Abla dostun nectnol stazeb."

You stare at him in incomprehension. He walks over and slaps you in the face. He had said, in whatever language, "Pass the salt or I will hit you."

How unfair is this? And yet every day, all over the world, riders do just that to their horses. They ask for something that the horse doesn't comprehend and then punish the horse when he fails to deliver the desired response.

So, the first principle: The rider and the horse have to speak the same "language."

Different types and styles of riding and training use different words to describe this communication between a human and a horse. "Aids" is one such word, often associated with English riding. "Cues" is another, more associated with Western riding. It doesn't matter what word we use, because whether it is "aids" or "cues" or "signals," what we are describing is nonverbal communication between a human and a horse.

Sure, there are some verbal stimuli, such as a cluck to go, or a "Whoa" to slow down, but most of the way we talk to a horse is with pressure and release, stimulus and response.

So, to ask a horse to go forward, we may cluck, press with our heels, tap with a stick. These are all "words" that are saying, "Horse, go forward." When the horse "replies" by going forward, we back off the pressures that we used to get him to go.

Think it through. First, we apply a certain stimulus that has a desired result, in this case to get the horse to go. Then, in response to the stimulus, the horse goes forward. Then, to "reward" the horse for replying to the stimulus, the rider ceases or, at least, softens the pressure that caused the horse to respond.

Simple, right? Instead of using our mouths to say "Go," we have used leg pressure or stick pressure. Then when the pressure created the desired result, instead of saying, "Thank you," with our mouths, we say, "Thank you," by softening the pressure. We are using other body parts to talk with the horse instead of using our mouths the way we would when speaking to another human.

Just Like Teaching a First-Grader

Now, just as a little kid doesn't know at first how to read or to write or to spell, the horse doesn't understand at the beginning what our various pressures are asking him to do.

Let's go back to the little human child in kindergarten or in first grade. The teacher doesn't expect the youngster to understand anything that is even slightly complex before the child has learned the more readily understood, simple things first. In reading, the teacher starts with A, B, C and D—the letters of the alphabet. In arithmetic, she starts with 1, 2, 3, 4—the numbers. She doesn't ask a six-year-old to spell "adversarial." But she might try to get him to spell "cat." She won't ask, "Kathy, what do you get if you add 357 to 926?" She might ask, "What do we get if we add 1 plus 1? Or 2 plus 2?"

> Just as a little kid doesn't know at first how to read or to write or to spell, the horse doesn't understand at the beginning what our various pressures are asking him to do.
>
> ■ ■ ■

First, a child must learn the individual letters and numbers, then simple little combinations to make simple little words, or to solve simple little problems.

With horses, to avoid all those awful struggles, all the tension, all the adversarial relationships that we so often see, it is the same basic way. Think of a mild tug on the right rein as "letter A." A mild tug on the left rein as "letter B." A pressure from our right leg as "letter C," and so on. We are teaching the alphabet to the horse so that he calmly understands what we are asking him to do.

When he responds to letter A by looking to the right, we release the pressure. When he moves left from our right leg, we release the pressure. We are not "making" him give to the pressure. We are teaching him that when he does give to the pressure, he will get relief from the stimulus.

When to Apply Pressure

One mistake that I used to make was to increase the pressure too soon if the horse didn't respond quickly enough. Let's say I applied my right leg to his flank to ask him to move his haunches to the left. And let's say I used fairly light pressure to get this to happen. Well, if I didn't get a quick response, I would use my leg again, but this time I would probably give him a little kick. If he still didn't move, I would give him a harder kick. Then a harder kick. Sooner or later, he would move away from the discomfort of my kicking leg.

The problem with this tactic of "escalating" the force of the request is that while I did get my horse to move away from my leg, there was too much fear and discomfort involved. By banging on his side with my heel or spur, I was getting him to give to the pressure, but at the same time I was making him anxious and nervous. Sure, I was winning the battle, but I was losing the war. What I mean by "losing the war" is that a tense horse has other issues that are worse than the piece I was trying to fix. A tense horse gets too strong, say. So now I have to use more hand to restrain him. So now my horse gets even more nervous because I am hanging on his mouth.

The harder I try, the more tight he gets, so the harder I try, and now the whole thing is like that old saying, "Going to hell in a hand basket." And I was the one who started the downhill slide by using an aid that was too strong.

The use of stronger, harsher bits, or draw reins, or other leverage devices, comes from not understanding how to create conditioned responses through "gentle pester" rather than sharp demand.

■ ■ ■

So, how should I have obtained the response? He didn't listen to my light leg pressure. Why shouldn't I use more if he fails to respond? Well, because of what I just said. Harder and harder pressure makes him more nervous. The way to get him to move is not to bang on his sides, but to "pester" him until he moves.

I have never read any book about riding that talks about "pestering" a horse. They always use the terms like "apply the aids," as if the horse will magically understand what the heck that means.

But think. Why does a horse switch his tail at a fly? Because the horse knows that the fly will bite him if he doesn't get rid of the damn thing. The horse is not terrified by the fly. The fly isn't an attacking mountain lion. It isn't even a stinging wasp. It's a fly. Even an annoying fly will get a horse to respond, but it is not a panicked response.

In a way, we riders need to be mildly annoying flies. We need to gently pester the horse. We need to mildly annoy the horse. Sure, the horse books don't say "pester" or "annoy," but what else are we doing? Does the horse want to move his haunches away from our legs? Does he want to pick up a right lead canter? No. He wants to be left alone in his pasture to eat grass with his friends.

So back to teaching the horse to move left from my right leg. I apply a little pressure on his right side, behind the girth. Nothing happens. He just stands there like a stone statue. So I gently poke him again. Still no response. Everything in my being is saying, "Kick the damn horse. Make him obey!"

But I know where that will lead, right? He'll move away, but I will have created tension. So I poke him again. And again. His ears maybe go back. I am annoying him—not scaring him, but annoying him—to the point that he notices me. I repeat my little aid. He steps away from my leg. I stop.

In a few seconds, here comes my leg again, pester, pester. When he moves away, the pestering ceases. In a week of doing this, right leg to move left, left leg to move right, my horse is starting to get the picture. Two plus two is starting to become four for him. I am building in a conditioned response.

A man who was giving elephant rides at the King Brothers' Circus had trained not only elephants but also big cats, bears, dogs, seals—you name it. Someone asked, "Do you train them all the same way?" And he said, "All but the dogs and seals. When the dog does the right thing I flip him a biscuit, and when the seal does the right thing, I flip him a fish. All the others, when they do what I want, I take off the pressure."

I've heard this described as "programming a computer." An untrained horse is an "unprogrammed computer." We are "installing buttons." The key is that we are installing those buttons calmly and consistently rather than roughly and forcefully.

There was a Greek king and general, in ancient times, whose name was Pyrrhus. In some battle against the Romans, the king's troops won, but half the army was lost. In the next battle, they were conquered by the Romans. So there came to be a term, "Pyrrhic victory," to describe what happens when someone wins a battle, but loses the war. That's what I used to have, lots of Pyrrhic victories. By using aids that were too forceful, I would get my horse to move away from my leg, or give to my hand, but from fear, pain, duress, rather than from conditioned response. The nervous anxiety that my horse would have because of my rough aids made him almost impossible to train unless I just kept adding force to force to force.

Once you go the tough route, it starts that terrible downward spiral. Rider force creates horse fear. Horse fear creates horse resistance. Horse resistance creates rider anger. Rider anger creates more force. You can see too well where this is going. The next thing will be stronger, harsher bits, or draw reins, or other leverage devices, and it all started with my not understanding how to create conditioned responses through "gentle pester" rather than sharp demand.

In order for us, as riders who are also trainers, to be able to teach all these conditioned responses, to install these various buttons, to program these living computers, we have to be able to use the same sets of stimulus and release each time (fig. 3.1).

Knowing How to Spell "Cat"

A first grade teacher always spells "cat" C-A-T. She doesn't spell it C-A-T and then K-A-T and then K-E-T and then C-A-P. No, it's always C-A-T if she wants the little six-year-olds to understand.

Extrapolate this to teaching a horse how to do a turn on the forehand to the right. We want his front legs to stay pretty much in the same place, but we want his hind end to pirouette to the right. So we bring our left leg, foot, maybe a little spur, back behind the girth, about 3 or 4 inches, and give him a little nudge. If he starts to move forward, we close our fingers on the reins. He takes a step or two to the right. We stop. "Good boy." Now we ask again. A couple more steps. "Good boy."

But we always try to use pretty much the same degree of pressure in pretty much the same place in pretty much the same direction every time we ask. We always want to spell cat C-A-T for our horse.

3.1: Great trainers like Jane Savoie are gifted athletes, but that is only where their excellence begins. Of greater importance, they bring empathy, compassion, and a host of technical and intellectual skills to the mission of creating finished products from green beginnings. Here she is riding Moshi.

All these aids that we use to "talk" to our horse are pressure specific, exactly as different words are specific. If I want you to pass me the salt, I will say, "Please pass the salt." I won't say, "Please pass the sugar." Don't speak German to someone who knows only French.

We are teaching our horse a language, and we can't teach a language that we don't know how to speak ourselves. So first, we need to know how to spell "cat." We have to know that two plus two equals four, because the essence of horse training, from the simplest "words" to the most complex sentences, depends on this pressure-release, stimulus-response system. It is really that simple. It is really that complex.

Nobody ever explained that to me. Or, if they did, I was too ignorant or too arrogant to grasp it.

The "Hot" Horse vs. the "High" Horse

When I was a kid, a local dealer told me that if a horse was "hot" it generally meant scared and reactive. If a horse was "high" it meant that the horse had lots of extra energy.

He said that it was lots easier to deal with one that was *high* because you could do things to get rid of the excess energy, like keep him in steady work, cut down on his grain, let him live out, but *hot* horses would often get hotter when worked, because getting worked only made them more nervous.

You can make a hot horse tired, in other words, but you are not getting rid of the nervousness that made him hot in the first place. It is hard to tell which is which, because, for the average rider, high horses and hot horses seem equally hard to deal with. (And probably should not be ridden by anyone who gets nervous and tight when a horse feels reactive, because all that does is ramp up the problem.)

So many riders get a young or green or worried horse and cannot *wait* to start training him. So they put the horse under more pressure than he can readily handle, and surprise, surprise, the horse gets harder to ride.

So surprise, surprise, they increase the pressure to fix the problem that their use of pressure already caused. And surprise, surprise, it gets worse, and the downward spiral has begun.

If people would just take the time it takes, and be calm and soft and less aggressive, there would be far fewer messed up horses. Say I, who did it the wrong way for years and years. But it's better to learn late than never.

> If people would just take the time it takes, and be calm and soft and less aggressive, there would be far fewer messed up horses.
>
> ■ ■ ■

Tone of Voice in Training

In human language, "tone of voice" can completely change the message.

Take this simple exchange between, say, a teenage girl and her mother. The mother asks the daughter to do something. The kid replies, in a cheerful tone of voice, "Yes, Mom." Or in a totally sarcastic tone, "YES, MOM," that implies that the request was the stupidest thing ever uttered in human history.

In just such a way the "tone" of a rider's aids can be mild and pleasant, or sharp and adversarial.

In order not to create anxiety or resistance, the good trainer keeps her "tone of voice" (read: intensity of physical stimuli) within certain limits, at least most of the time. Sure, there are sometimes situations that require a shout, but shouting should be reserved for when it is really needed. If a rider stops a horse by always yanking on the reins, which is analogous to always shouting in a harsh tone, this will create a tense, worried, anxious horse.

The Fine Art of Puttering

To "putter" means to sort of dub around in a seemingly mindless manner, without a goal or an agenda or being on a mission. Puttering means a little of this, a little of that, no straight line in sight, no expected conclusion, not much in the way of conscious thought.

General synonyms for puttering around might include fiddling around, messing around, or tinkering around.

Now I am perfectly aware that most horse books about training horses might suggest that the essence of training is to have an agenda of some sort leading to a goal of some sort, and I don't mean to suggest that those books have it all wrong.

The horses that benefit from puttering, though, are apt to be tense and nervous, horses that have already been "agenda-ized" to the hilt. Somehow, somewhere, someone took these horses and probably tried to fit the square peg into the round hole, and when the horse resisted, the rider probably ratcheted up the intensity of the training. For horses like this, the beauty of puttering is that the rider is

Carrie Ramsey on Beaulieu's Cool Concorde: Carrie is asking Cordi for a light stretch, which will be followed by a release.

"saying" to the horse, "I know you are anxious. I realize that you are distrustful. So I am not going to add to your nervousness. Instead, I want you to start to understand that you can unwind and take a deep breath."

If the horse you are training seems to wind up rather than to wind down in work, try puttering your way toward your goal, tiny pressures on, tiny pressures swiftly released.

In Praise of Walking

In 1955, when I was first getting involved in distance riding, I read an article in the Green Mountain Horse Association magazine that had some title like, "In Praise of Walking."

As I was 13 or 14, I had not yet heard about the concept of "long slow distance" as the underlying base for all kinds of later, faster, and more rigorous work, but the article said that the safest and most reliable way to build basic strength and soundness was to take the horse for active daily walks, and to fundamentally walk the horse into shape (fig. 3.2).

Another point the article made, "It is very unlikely that you will injure a horse at the walk." Many riders do not get this simple concept. They may not

3.2: "It is hard to injure a horse at a walk." This was something I was taught early on, and I have found walking to be a foundation for so much else that we do with horses. (This is Meet In Khartoum, an OTTB mare whose sibling was American Pharoah, a horse not known for his speed at a walk!)

have the space and place for long, vigorous walks. They may feel they lack the time. They may find walking boring and unproductive.

Whatever the reason, it seems that many horses are pushed into training before they have been given a solid base of physical fitness and strength that will allow them to handle the training without distress, and that is simply bad horsemanship.

Try not to go there. Be smarter and more patient than that. Be fair to the horse. First, get him fit, and then add to that. It is actually an incredibly simple concept.

Simple Sheer Physical Strength

I am going to go out on a limb here and say that the single most mis-understood training concept is the extent to which creating physical strength, power, and fitness in a horse can totally transform that animal into an elite athlete, in a way that not only changes the physical abilities, but also has a huge impact on what we often call the "character" of a horse—his willing-ness to try, his courage, his degree of true grit, that thing we call "heart."

We see this in human athletes as well, an almost "arrogant" sense of well-being in the highly conditioned, sleek, and muscular runners; boxers; soccer, football, and hockey players; swimmers; skiers; men and women who look more like those statues of Greek gods than mere mortals.

Taking our OTTB Rosie's Girl, as an example, when we got her fresh off a failed racing career at four years old, she was one of those slight, even what you might call "weedy" Thoroughbred fillies. We walked her for many, many long slow miles, both on Vermont hills, and through the miles of sandy trails in the Southern Pines, North Carolina, Walthour-Moss Foundation.

Little by little, Rosie began to change in her general appearance—not in terms

Strength and Fitness

Anything that an athlete can even begin to do while weak and unfit, he can do much more easily and far more successfully when strong and fit. This would seem to be a total no-brainer, but based on what we so often see, it somehow slides right by too many riders and trainers.

One of the easiest ways to understand this concept is to apply it to humans (fig. 3.3). Go downtown, any downtown, any place, and randomly pick 25 human adults. Drag them, kicking and screaming, down to the local high school athletic fields. Make them run a mile.

Rosie's Girl with Daryl Kinney

became easy as she developed the fit physique to keep tiredness at bay.

I can almost promise you that if you have a horse that is sound enough to handle the gradually increasing work load, and if you have the time and dedication to put into stacking up that degree of mileage, you will be building a horse that will bear little resemblance to the one you started with, and not just in physical appearance. The creation of simple, sheer physical strength comes as close to "magic" as any training strategy ever developed.

of getting much bigger, because skeletal structure is what it is, but in terms of what was there becoming hard, strong muscle tone. And, as Rosie got stronger, and gained stamina and endurance, she got braver. The exertions that used to cause discomfort and stress simply

3.3: You can't do 10 pushups if you can't do seven. You can't do seven if you can't do four. Sometimes a horse is so weak that he can't do the equivalent of one pushup. Start at the beginning. Build on that. Human or horse, as Nathan Merchant demonstrates.

What are you going to see? We know what we are going to see. Puffing, panting, wheezing, sweating, gasping—let's just say, "It ain't gonna be pretty!"

Unless, by sheer accident we plucked a marathon runner out of the office, the average human adult is a distant reflection of the way he or she looked back in high school when he or she was on the basketball team.

But because a horse starts out as bigger, stronger, and faster than a human, it's easy to assume that horses are immune to the same deleterious effects of lethargy and inactivity that so badly afflict our 25 random off-the-street human selections.

A soft, unfit, under-exercised horse will be just as unable to perform at a decent athletic level as his human counterpart, but many riders seem not to get that. They will saddle up for a joy ride on Saturday morning and go galloping around on some poor horse whose normal maximum exertion is wandering from one end of his small paddock to the other, or far worse, from one side of his 10 by 10 foot stall to the other.

Joy ride for whom? Sure as shooting, not for the panting, sweating, struggling horse. We all need to get real. There is only one way for any organism to get fit—human, dog, horse, or guppy. It is that horrible, terrible, awful, to-be-avoided-at-all-costs word, "E-X-E-R-C-I-S-E."

In endurance and distance riding, there are two sets of initials that we see frequently in conditioning articles: "LSD" and "SFD." These stand for "long slow distance" and "short fast distance." The key idea is that the first, the longer, slower miles, build the base so that by the time the horse is asked to do shorter, faster work, he is fit and strong and able to do so without getting hurt.

Humans know from all kinds of workouts—running, biking, hiking up hills, carrying boxes upstairs—that there are different "systems," which all feel the stress of activity. When we run, we pant. This is our "respiratory system" trying to get more oxygen. Our hearts beat faster. We are pumping more oxygen. This is our cardiovascular system. Our muscles hurt. If we do too much we can sprain an ankle or tear a muscle, or rip a tendon or a ligament.

It's exactly the same for a horse. The tired horse pants and gets soaked with sweat. His heart races. And he becomes at heightened risk of muscle, ligament, and tendon injuries.

And here's the thing about tendon and ligament injuries. They stop a horse in his tracks, take months and months to heal, if they ever do, and at worst, can end his athletic career forever. To put this bluntly, you do not want

> A soft, unfit, under-exercised horse will be just as unable to perform at a decent athletic level as his human counterpart.

your horse to bow a tendon or get an injured suspensory ligament. A bowed tendon will take a year, at least, to fully heal, a suspensory can take as long, and either one can be career-limiting or career-ending.

If you don't want these injuries to happen, be sure that you have built such a strong base of steady, slow, incremental work into your horse that his various systems—heart, lungs, muscles, tendons, bones, hooves—can withstand the forces put on them by exercise.

The way to start "long slow distance" is by walking your horse. When he is totally unfit, maybe start with 30 minutes for a couple of weeks, four to five days a week. Then build to, say, 45 minutes of walking for five to six days a week for a couple more weeks. Once you have given your horse a month to six weeks of walking, you can start to add some trotting.

A couple of things to think about: There is the brisk "get on down the road" kind of active walk, the "slothful shuffle" where the horse sort of drags one lethargic leg after another, and various gradations in between. You are going to get a lot more done in terms of building fitness if your walk is a brisk march instead of an amble. A lot of this will depend on the rider, and whether the rider has any gear, or just sits there like a toad.

There's an old story about a cavalry sergeant who comes up to his captain. "That hoss you got walks so fast all the men behind you, they gotta jig their hosses just to keep up."

The captain replies, "Sergeant, bring me the slowest walking plug in the regiment." The sergeant obliges, dragging behind him a reluctant plodder.

A week goes by and the sergeant reappears. "Hey, Captain. That hoss you got walks so fast all the men behind you, they gotta jig their hosses just to keep up."

If your horse is an ambler, chances are that you let him amble. Make him go. If he jigs, make him come back to a walk, then push him again to walk on. He'll get the picture, but you have to paint the picture for him, not just sit there like an inert lump.

3.4: Many riders find walking boring. Many riders do not have land to walk on. Many riders lack understanding of the enormous benefits that come from "LSD"—long slow distance. Which leads to an unfortunate conclusion: lots of horses hardly ever get walked into fitness. Here I am, on Roxie, walking my way home—six miles to go.

It's Hard to Injure a Horse at the Walk

So I repeat, "It's very hard to injure a horse at a walk." Sure, he can get a girth rub at a walk or a saddle sore. He can step on a rock and get a sole bruise. He can get tired and sore from endless walks. But those traumatic, tearing, wrenching injuries usually result from speeds beyond the 3 to 4 miles-an-hour of the walk (fig. 3.4).

Learn the secret weapon of the walk. My guess is that riders don't use the walk as a safe body-building strategy for several reasons. One, people say, "I don't have time to waste by just walking. I need (or want) to get more accomplished."

Another reason is that, frankly, walking can seem appallingly boring compared to trotting, cantering, galloping, or jumping. Riders may suspect that they are pushing the unfit horse past safe limits, but they are unwilling to take the time to put in the boring hours of creating the fitness base.

A big reason for this, in twenty-first-century America (and many other places), is that there isn't much available land at the farm where they ride. And, let's face it, boring becomes even more boring when it consists of making 142 consecutive loops around a two-and-a-half-acre field, or worse, 367 consecutive loops around an outdoor ring, or even worse, 472 loops around an indoor ring to get in the requisite number of minutes of walking that will begin to take "El Flabbo" and start the transformation to "El Magnifico," the dream horse of sleek coat and rippling musculature.

Now any good Pony Club maven will tell you that you should never, ever ride with headphones, earbuds, whatever, but one way to alleviate the tedium of churning out those walking miles, assuming you are not riding in some beautiful forest or state park where you are anything but bored, is to get a good playlist of songs that you like, crank up the volume, and never tell your Pony Club teacher, on the sure assumption that what she doesn't know can't hurt her.

Faster Work When Ready

At some point, depending on how unfit your horse was when you began your walking fitness regimen, it will be time to add some trotting.

I don't think you need to be as super-scientific as some books or fitness programs suggest, such as, "Start with three three-minute trots for the first four days. Skip one day, and add another three-minute trot set on the fourth day—and so on."

I am not opposed to using this type of highly systematic approach, but if your situation doesn't lend itself to that much regimentation, or if your personality rebels at the sheer "math" of such systems, just use common sense.

You have built your horse a fitness base by increasingly longer walks, and now you are going to add to that base by doing some trotting. You can tell if you are overdoing it. He will start to pant and sweat, and it will take him a while to catch his breath when you come back to a walk. "Hey," you will say. "Sorry, buddy. I didn't know this was too much. I'll back off, and give you more time to get ready for more intensity."

Jack Le Goff, my coach when I was riding for the USET Three-Day Team, used to say, "Listen to your horse." You will start to get better and better at reading the signals that are the only ways that a horse can tell you how he is feeling and how he is doing. We've already talked about some of the more obvious ways, such as heavy, sustained panting, profuse sweating, and increasing reluctance to go forward—all signs that he's sort of had it. But there are other clues, once you learn to look. How hot is it out? How humid? How deep or firm or rough is the footing? Are there hills that you are asking him to climb? If so, how steep are they, and how sustained? All these variables will play into whether what you ask is okay with your horse, or whether it is causing him distress.

> You will start to get better and better at reading the signals that are the only ways that a horse can tell you how he is feeling and how he is doing.
>
> ■ ■ ■

When Jack Le Goff urged us to "listen" to our horses, he didn't mean just with our ears. He wanted us to tune in to them in all sorts of ways: how they felt while hacking out, while galloping, while climbing hills, while standing at rest. Is this a bright, happy horse, or a lethargic horse? One with energy or one who seems spent?

If we study horses, rather than just look at them without really seeing, we can learn to read all these signs. It's a big part of what makes the difference between a horseman or horsewoman and a man or woman who has horses.

Pretty Good, Good, and Quit While You're Ahead

When training horses, "pretty good" needs to be seen as "good," and "quit while you're ahead" should be everyone's motto.

It is so easy to grind on a horse, to make the horse do something, perform a specific movement, then do it again, and again, and again, all the way to frustration, fatigue, failure, and despair.

We see this every day. Heck, we do this every day. Perfection is the curse of the perfectionist. "Practice doesn't make perfect. Perfect practice makes perfect." How often have we had this saying shoved down our throats? As if to hear something enough times somehow makes it true.

The Curse of Perfectionism

Walk-to-canter, canter-to-walk transitions are hard, so this is a good example. The horse inverts in the upward transition, say, or takes too many trot steps in the downward transition. So it's not good enough. So we do it again. The horse does it sort of okay. But, no, sort of okay is not good enough. Do it again. Now the horse is starting to get a little worried. Or tired. Or worried and tired. So he gets "resistant." Now, by God, it's really not good enough. So we do it again. And once more....

See where this is going? It is going to hell in a hand basket, that's where it's going. It can now only end badly, with a mentally and physically fried horse and an angry and frustrated human.

If we had let the "pretty good" equal good, and quit with that, we'd have been so far ahead. We could have ended with a calm horse, not one who feels as though he has been put through the wringer.

Many days of "pretty good" start to add up to quite good indeed. Grinding to perfection gives the opposite result. It's a hard lesson for many riders to learn. I wish I had learned it about 40 years sooner.

Getting Mad at a Horse

We've all watched it. If we were bluntly honest, most of us have done it. The "it" in question is losing our temper with a horse. Some riders almost never get exasperated enough to get rough with a horse, and for some riders, getting into "World War III" is something that happens just about every time they ride.

If getting angry enough to get rough with a horse just never happens in your situation, consider yourself one of the fortunate ones. You can probably just skip this entire section. But most of us are not that saintly, and one way to alleviate the adversarial struggles that leave both rider and horse "fried"—upset, scared, or angry—is to try to figure out why people get mad at horses.

> Many days of "pretty good" start to add up to quite good indeed.
>
> ■ ■ ■

I think we have to acknowledge that some people are just angry. People who carry around lots of anger get into it with other people, with their family members, with their dogs, while driving their cars, at work—and getting mad at a horse is just one more manifestation of that deeply brewing hostility. These are scary people, to be avoided as much as possible, because the anger within bubbles near the surface and it doesn't take much for that anger to lash out at whatever or whomever happens to do anything to provoke it. If one of these angry people owns horses, trains horses, runs a stable, teaches riding, shoes horses, or has any interactions with horses or the people around those horses, it's pretty much guaranteed to be a tense, unhappy barn or farm.

Then there are those who just don't "get it" that horses are flight animals who don't like loud noise, quick movement, abrupt handling, being kicked, yanked, chased, admonished, and punished for "bad" behavior.

People who are sort of clueless about how to behave around horses make horses nervous and flighty and reactive. Then, when the horse does get reactive, the clueless non-horse people often tend to chastise the horse for the behavior that they caused in the first place.

The way forward with these people is to try to explain to them why their horses don't basically trust them. Some will learn better ways, and some won't. We all know the saying, "You can't fix stupid."

Some people get angry and rough because they are scared. We see this scenario most frequently with riders who have horses that are "too much horse" for their ability and confidence level. The rider trots down the road, and the horse spooks at a mailbox. Yank, spur, "Don't be a brat!" yells the nervous rider. The horse feels the spur, feels the yank, hears the sharp yell. Is he going to calm down? No way. He's going to get more nervous. This scares and provokes the rider even more. Her "aids" get more abrupt and sharp. The horse gets more upset. You don't have to be Albert Einstein to see where this is headed.

Some people get angry and rough when they think that the horse they are riding is being willfully disobedient. These riders say things like, "He knows what I want him to do, but he just won't do it." Or things like, "This horse is being a pig." Or things like, "My horse is such a jerk." The list goes on.

The reality, almost always, is that the horse doesn't understand what the rider wants, hasn't been trained to perform the requested task, hasn't had the aid applied correctly, or isn't strong enough to do what the rider wants.

It all starts with the rider saying, "My horse won't do what I want."

The Warm-Up

Jack Le Goff called the warm-up "gymnasticizing" the horse. "Warming up" a horse means different things to different riders, and this will often depend on what the horse will be asked to do.

If you are going for a trail ride and you spend the first 15 to 20 minutes at a walk, this is probably a pretty decent preparation for adding in some trotting. Now, by "walk" I don't mean some moribund shuffle, but a nice getting-along active walk that stretches the topline, gets the heart going, gets

3.5: "Long and low" is a go-to exercise for many top trainers who realize the enormous benefits of the elastic athlete. Here Carrie Ramsey asks Cordi to drop her head "from the withers" to lift her back and lengthen the degree of swing out of her shoulders. "Never bounce or force a stretch" is the truism to remember about anything involving the "gymnasticizing" benefits of elongating the range of motion of muscle fibers.

the blood pumping and the lungs breathing, not to excess, but enough to be a transition between standing around and more vigorous exercise (fig. 3.5).

Unfortunately for me, in my early years, I watched too many Western movies. The cowboy comes out of the saloon, unties his horse from the hitching rail, hops on, and canters down Main Street.

I don't think I was quite that bad, but I didn't have a clue about loosening up tight muscles or how too short a warm-up fails to get through to a horse's mental state to help make him calm and relaxed in the work. I guess a good human example is when the Marine drill instructor flips on the barracks lights at four in the morning and rousts the recruits out of bed so they can go on a nice run in the cold, rainy dark. The humans hate it, and your horse won't like it any better if you don't give him time to gradually make the physical and emotional switch from doing nothing to any sort of vigorous exercise.

Part of the warm-up that I didn't understand is the whole concept of stretching the muscles, tendons, and ligaments, and how tricky this can be to do correctly and without creating pain and real structural damage.

There are all kinds of sayings about what *not* to do while stretching: "Don't force a stretch." "Don't bounce a stretch." "Don't stretch to the point of real pain." All of these "don'ts" are based on the reality that muscle fibers can get stretched to the point that they can tear and rupture. A torn muscle stops any athlete in his tracks. Muscle tears cause intense pain, and they limit all sorts of physical activity, so you don't want to go there.

If you wouldn't want it done to you, don't do it to a horse.

■ ■ ■

The way to create an increased range of motion through stretching is to think of bringing the muscle to a point of some tension, mildly uncomfortable, but no more than that, holding the stretch for a number of seconds, and then releasing the tension. It's create tension, hold tension, release tension. Be careful, careful, careful. Better to underdo than to overdo. Little by little, day by day, week by week, this is the way to increase range of motion.

Some riders and so-called "trainers" feel that a horse "refuses" to stretch, and they drag out the draw reins and other leverage devices to force the horse to stretch beyond his ability to do so, causing pain, distress, and real physical damage. This is not only bad training, it is real cruelty. Damn well don't do it. It reminds me of the way torturers used to put human prisoners on the rack, pulling their bodies into agony. If you wouldn't want it done to you, don't do it to a horse.

Riding Hours a Week: The Huge Challenge for Amateurs

Most riders, I'm pretty sure, don't have an exact record of how many hours each week they actually spend riding any given horse. As a result and as I've mentioned, I'd bet most horses are less than fully fit and well conditioned for the tasks they are expected to perform.

We've now discussed the mantra stating that LSD (long, slow distance) miles are the basic building blocks of fitness, and that these slow miles should have been thoroughly "installed" before we ask for SFD (short, fast distance). This is because unless hooves, bones, and muscles—the structures that support tendons and ligaments—have been hardened, we put those tendons and ligaments at higher risk. We all know about the enormous damage done to young racehorses, and one major reason for this is that most Thoroughbreds get galloped for fitness, but few go for long walks, over weeks and months of time, before speed is introduced. (There are other causes, like being too young to begin with.)

There are all kinds of reasons that riders shortchange their horses on the basics of fitness. One is a true lack of available riding time, especially for those who try to squeeze in an hour before or after work or school. Another is that what we may think we do is different from what we really do. Let's say that we plan to ride for one hour. We have to go get the horse. Then we have to groom him, assemble the tack, and tack him up. Then we go to wherever we get on. Now, let's assume that we were planning to ride from about five to six in the evening. Did we actually get on at five? Very often not, I'll bet. One "short phone call" or some other "quick" interruption, and 5 minutes, 10 minutes are gone in a flash, so now it's 5:12 and we're not yet in the saddle.

Now we start to ride, and we do whatever it is we were planning to do, but there's a warm-up period, and a cool-down process, and perhaps we get off to walk the horse out at 5:55—well, that's a cumulative 17 minutes of our riding "hour" when no riding takes place. Repeat that two or three times a week, and if we ride five days a week, that horse gets what, about four hours each week of actual riding? He probably should get about double that to really address the fitness issue.

Another reason so many riders don't hack out, don't go for hour-and-a-half rides, is that they are stuck on some postage-stamp piece of land where it just isn't possible. Traffic and congestion is the new American reality in many places, and as I said earlier, who wants to circle one small field 47 times to get in 90 minutes of riding?

One thing I've started doing is making a log of my riding hours. I have three horses in work: two coming-six-year-old Warmblood mares and a coming-six-year-old Morgan mare, and my goal is to average 80 minutes of actual riding time per horse, six days a week, which is 8 hours a week per horse. Some days I ride all three; many days Natalie Klein rides one while I ride another. But we are getting the work done, and all three mares look good, and feel great, and they are clearly very much fitter and stronger than they were a few months ago.

> **Most horses are less than fully fit and well conditioned for the tasks they are expected to perform.**
>
> ■ ■ ■

There's no one magic formula, apart from that well-established old saying, "LSD precedes SFD." Start writing down your actual hours of riding, and do this for several weeks. Perhaps you'll be pleasantly surprised at how much you are riding, or maybe you'll be disappointed, but either way, you'll have something reality-based as your litmus test.

I know so many people who have an almost endless number of reasons to avoid riding the horse that is sitting in the barn or in the field. And while it isn't the end of the world if a horse misses a day, or if the rider doesn't feel like fighting cold weather, or a head cold, or some other legitimate reason, here might be something to consider: lethargy breeds lethargy, sloth breeds sloth, and the less one does, the less one feels like doing, in an endless downward spiral turning into one of the best descriptions of all time, "The Blob That Ate Chicago"—for both horse and rider.

Every Ride Is a Training Opportunity

So this is one reason to make yourself go ride. Another is that every ride is a training ride.

A case in point was a hack that several of us from our barn had not long ago: Carrie Ramsey on Portada, Adriana Terleckyj on Moon, and me on Meet In Khartoum, all three OTTBs, Khartoum and Portada not yet quite six years old.

Portada was in front, and we were approaching the scary narrow bridge with a pile of equally scary logs off in the weeds on the side of the trail. Portada stopped dead. Just behind her, my mare stopped dead, stared at a dark log end sticking into the trail and started backing up rapidly, eventually bumping into Moon.

I tapped Khartoum with my whip, tap-tap, and she went forward maybe three steps, then five or six backward, up a little bank. I repeated the tap. Khartoum retreated. I let her stare. Portada just stood there, also staring—a little woodland tableau of two stuck OTTBs. Moon was not quite stuck yet, because he had not yet spotted the terrifying log. Probably Portada would go, but I wanted to see if I could get Khartoum unstuck on her own.

Eventually, when it was becoming clear that the only way I might get Khartoum to move was to really smack her, which would probably cause her to kick back at Moon, I said to Carrie, "See if Portada will go."

Portada, neck arched, walked by the log; Khartoum followed. When I got next to the log, I turned Khartoum to face it on the side of the trail. She took a step toward it, head down, nostrils wide, backed up, and stopped. For maybe a minute, I let her stand. Then, kick, tap, I asked her to go forward. This time she put her nose down all the way, and physically touched the log, sniffed it, chilled out, and walked by.

So that might have taken three to four minutes, maybe five. We could have simply let the braver ones go first from the get-go, but then Khartoum would have only gone by because she was protected by the others, not because she had learned anything.

But she *did* learn something—a lot more than if she had been standing in her field back at the farm with Roxie and Thistle eating grass.

Ride the horse for fitness; ride the horse for his education.

Riding Clinics: What You Should, and Should Not, Expect

"No man is a hero to his valet." That old saying pertains to the truism that prolonged access to even the most brilliant people draws a shutter of familiarity upon that brilliance. To us, Winston Churchill was the man who saved Western civilization. It may be apocryphal, but it has been said that, to his valet, he was a grumpy old man who scattered his clothes on the floor.

That is why Gold Medal Rider A can conduct a clinic in the home territory of Gold Medal Rider B, while Gold Medal Rider B can conduct a clinic in the home territory of Rider A. Neither will fill a clinic nearer home, because the luster of new and different has worn off.

If you decide to take your horse to a clinic, it's a good idea to realize what a clinic is and what a clinic is not.

The "not" part is simple. You are not going to magically learn how to ride at a clinic. No clinician comes to town with a "Good Riding Fairy" in his or her pocket, complete with the magic wand that can tap you on the shoulder and endow you with skills and knowledge previously not acquired. It's just not going to happen, because learning how to ride well takes years of study and practice.

So what can you expect to take away from a clinic? The answer to this will depend on how much skill and expertise you are bringing to the clinic (fig. 3.6). The more you already know, the better you can already ride, the more you can avail yourself of new concepts and strategies and riding techniques.

If you are still learning how to post on the correct diagonal, trying to figure out how to get your horse onto the right or left lead at the canter, you

3.6: Former USET show jumper Bernie Traurig, on the right, teaching a clinic at our farm in Southern Pines, North Carolina, in April, 2008.

probably won't get anything from a clinic that you can't get even better from your regular local instructor.

Face reality, hard as that may be. Riding well is a building blocks sort of learning process, and the basic building blocks are something that most clinicians usually assume that you already have.

So the clinician, unless this clinic has been set up for the entry-level rider, will probably introduce various methods and concepts that assume a base-level skill from the participants. Typically, the clinic organizer will have asked you your level of proficiency so that she can put you in a group with those of about equal abilities. Be honest when you answer the questionnaire. If you are hard-pressed to jump 2 feet, please say so. If you are getting ready to move up to, say, riding over 3-foot-6-inch to 4-foot courses, and want and need the challenge, tell her that. The organizer's goal is to make the participants fit into the right groups, and she will need your truthful input.

The best way to ride in a clinic is with the blessing of your regular instructor, who will know that what you will hear is an extension of what you are already being taught. Many riders find it valuable to audit a clinic with an instructor before signing up to ride in the next one. Treat a clinic like a college lecture or series of lectures. Bring a notebook. Write things down. Pay attention. Don't just come to your session then leave for the day. A clinic is not a lesson. A good clinic will be a distillation of what the clinician has learned over many years. You can get that information only if you are open to learning, not if you are chatting and paying scant attention.

If a week goes by since the clinic, and someone asks you, "What did you learn at the Jim Smith clinic?" you'd better have some valid answers, or you wasted your money and squandered another opportunity to learn something.

Seeing a Distance

Imagine that you are watching a class at a jumper show. The first rider enters the ring, canters a warm-up circle, and proceeds toward the first jump. She gets the horse from an active but balanced canter to a spot about 6 feet in front of the jump, the place from which it is easiest for the horse to leave the ground and clear the obstacle. This 6-foot distance, give or take a little, isn't so close to the jump that the horse has trouble getting his knees up and out of the way in time before the highest rail, nor is it so far away that the horse has to either launch himself at the jump or put in a little short stride (called "chipping in"), which is the same as if he had gotten too close.

The rider proceeds to all the other jumps on the course, and gets her horse time after time to that optimum distance in front of each fence, thus giving her horse a good chance of clearing each jump.

There are all sorts of descriptions and phrases that define this skill. One is that she "has a good eye." Another is that she can "see her distance." Another, "She can get him in right." Another, "She can nail the spot." All these sayings are used to describe the rider whose horse rarely has to struggle to deal with being too close to or too far away from the jump that the horse is attempting to navigate.

Now into the ring comes the next rider. He chases the horse into a strung-out canter and arrives at a distance too far away from the first jump, say perhaps 8 or 9 feet in front as his last stride ends. The horse feels too insecure to attempt to jump from so far away from the fence, so in desperation, he adds a short stride, but now he is too close, somewhere about 3 or 4 feet in front, possibly even closer. At this point, the horse has three options, all bad.

> No clinician comes to town with a "Good Riding Fairy" in his or her pocket, complete with the magic wand that can tap you on the shoulder and endow you with skills and knowledge previously not acquired.
>
> ■ ■ ■

He can refuse the jump, also known as "stopping," because he feels incapable of clearing the fence from such a close distance. Option two: he tries to jump, but crashes through it. Option three: he can do a "helicopter" jump, sort of straight up and straight down, leaving the rails in the cups, but causing the horse great effort and probably significant worry.

Then, at the next fence, the horse gets to a pretty nice spot. Then too close. Then too long. Then too long. Then good. Then too short.

The rider who "lies" to his horse in this way, constantly causing the horse to struggle with bad distances, is said to "have no eye." Or he can't "see his distance." Or some other way of implying that he canters around the course like the blind man tapping along the sidewalk with a white cane.

It is an enormous advantage for a jumper rider to have a good eye for a distance, because he can help rather than hinder his horse to jump more easily. There are some trainers who actually say that a rider need not have a good eye because it is the job of the horse rather than the job of the rider to find the optimal takeoff spot every time in front of every jump. These trainers postulate that if the rider can create a nice active yet balanced canter, the horse will see his own distances and won't make mistakes where his own self-preservation is at stake.

This idea that it's "not your job to get in right, it's the horse's job," absolves the rider of the need to develop a good eye, but there is one fatal flaw in such a simplistic approach.

Seeing-Eye Horses

Some horses will get in right, almost like "seeing-eye" horses, but some won't. Some will save themselves (and their riders) time after time. Some will gallop on down and eat the jump. There are canny jumpers and there are klutzy jumpers. Anyone who has jumped dozens or hundreds of horses knows this. Some horses will find the distances and some won't. And some that find the distances some of the time will not always find the distances all of the time.

All of which leaves me with the conclusion that a rider with a good eye is in a much safer place than a rider with a bad eye—or "no eye," as it is sometimes phrased.

This leads to the next question, "Can a rider who can't see a distance *learn* to see a distance?"

I think the answer to this is "probably." So what does this mean? Well, let's think this through. I suspect that there are those riders with such superior binocular vision who can just "tell" whether they are right or wrong. They may not know if they are five strides away, or four strides, or six strides, but they can "just tell" if they are going to meet the distance perfectly, or if they need to shorten the stride or lengthen the stride to get to the best takeoff spot. For these rare riders simply "born" with a good eye, lucky them. They can skip the rest of this because they don't need to learn to see a distance some other way—they already *can* see it, almost as a "gift from God."

But most riders are not so blessed, not initially. They come cantering down to the fence like the guy calling his Dalmatian, "Here, Spot. Here, Spot." Most riders need to develop their eye another way, and here are some strategies that have worked for me, and for quite a few of those I've taught.

The first thing to understand is that you have to have an adjustable canter. The reason is simple. As your eye begins to develop, you will begin to recognize that if you keep cantering the same way, the jump will be just right, too close, or too far away. So let's just say that you are beginning to "recognize" what three strides in front of a fence looks like. You will need a canter that is adjustable enough to let you maintain it "as is" or lengthen it or shorten it, to get to that "6-feet-in-front-of-the-jump" perfect takeoff spot.

> Most riders come cantering down to a fence like the guy calling his Dalmatian, "Here, Spot. Here, Spot."
>
> ■ ■ ■

If your canter is too aggressively forward, you won't be able to shorten. If it's too lethargic, you won't be able to lengthen. You need what Jack Le Goff called "a canter that gives you access to both balance and impulsion." If you have too much impulsion, too "forward-bound" a canter, you can lengthen, but you can't shorten (see fig. 5.8, p. 198).

When balance, the feeling that your horse is up and light in front of you, has "throttled" the impulsion, you can shorten the stride, but you can't lengthen it. You need both. You need impulsion to go, but you need balance to whoa. Neither one alone is sufficient. It is easy to get one or the other. It is hard, hard, hard to have instant access to both at once. So, developing a feel for an adjustable canter becomes a major goal in your quest to achieve a good eye.

The Hoofprint Game

I think the best way to start to acquire an eye is to put out a bunch of rails in the ring, and start riding at a canter toward one, then another, then another, starting by thinking, "I'm going to get an accurate three-stride eye" (fig. 3.7).

3.7: Pick any fixed object that can substitute for a jump. Think of this as the "Hoofprint Game." Do this hundreds, thousands, tens of thousands of times, and your eye will get better and better and better. Guaranteed.

It's pretty simple. As you get closer to the rail on the ground, you simply take a guess that you are three strides away, and you say 3-2-1. You will either be just right, about 3 or 4 feet in front of the rail, so that a normal canter stride puts the rail under the middle of the "jump" stride, or you will be too close, or you will be too far away.

Then do it again at another rail. And again, and again, hundreds of times. Then thousands of times. At some point, you will begin to develop a sense of what three strides look like. Some riders get it almost instantly, while for others it takes a long time, but it will happen if you keep practicing.

You don't even need rails on the ground, because you can use hoofprints, dandelions in a field, pinecones on a trail, any fixed object that you are cantering toward. As your number of "jumps" gets higher, your sense of canter adjustability, as well as your sense of distance, will improve. This is because you can see a distance, perhaps, but until you can also adjust the canter, it doesn't do you any good to see it if you can't shorten or lengthen the stride enough to get there.

At first you will probably miss a lot, no big deal. But as dozens turn into hundreds, hundreds into thousands, thousands into tens of thousands, as months and years of practice go by, you will start to both see a distance and be able to create an adjustable canter.

It is a myth that you are either born with a good eye or you are not. When Daryl Kinney, our former barn manager, first came here 10 years ago, she did not have an eye. By doing this exercise, she got a three-stride eye. Then, with more practice, a four-stride eye. Watch her ride. She almost never misses by even a foot.

Most people, I promise you this, will read this and ignore it. They will not practice enough. But most people, in any endeavor, will not work hard enough to get good. It is all about choice.

Eight-Year Overnight Success

I half joke about Rosie's Girl and Daryl Kinney being an eight-year overnight success, but it is not actually joking.

Another piece of the building-blocks creation that is easily glossed over in this age of buying fancy and accomplished horses for young riders is just how many years of intense study and practice is involved in turning the human part of the equation into "equal shares," so to speak.

When Daryl started working for us about 10 years ago, she had not ridden above Training Level in eventing. I think that she would be the first to tell you that many, even most, of the riding skills she has today, she did not have then.

We read these stories of this and that young rider winning at higher levels, and I can almost guarantee that in most—not all, but most—of these instances, the child will have been underwritten with wonderful horses that have "Been there, done that."

Daryl and Rosie's Girl after about six years of schooling together.

When you do it from scratch, learning as the horse learns, it takes longer, but I believe that the skills we learn the hard, slow, thorough way, we will be likely to "own" in ways that those who had it easier—had the proverbial rose petals cast in their path—may never understand.

So if the struggle for you is real, that is not always the worst thing that can happen, if you are not easily beaten down or easily discouraged.

Becoming a Tuning Fork

An adjustable canter goes hand in glove with a good eye, so as you can see, you will need to develop a "sense of canter." I read a quotation years ago about the jumper rider Margie Goldstein-Engle that said, "Margie's body is a tuning fork for the right canter."

Most riders' bodies are not tuning forks for that adjustable canter, so there is a goal to strive for. Here comes the jump, three long strides away. Can you instantly lengthen the canter stride to get to the best takeoff point? Or you see that the three strides will get you too close to the jump, so can you instantly shorten the canter stride to give your horse more room to get his knees up?

These are skills "owned" by the better jumper riders, and whether they own them from birth or have struggled to acquire them, the fact remains that they can do two things: They can see the distance from three or four or even more strides away, and they can create an adjustable enough canter to be able to get there.

More on the Good Canter

It may seem redundant to keep talking about the good canter but it is important to understand it fully because so often it is the missing piece that should be in the arsenal of every jumping rider. Jack Le Goff harped on the good canter as being one that was a combination of two rather incompatible qualities: balance and impulsion.

To lengthen the stride, the canter needs impulsion.

To shorten the stride, the canter needs balance.

Too much impulsion, the horse usually goes forward and down. Now you can lengthen, but you can't shorten.

Too much balance, if you sort of nip, nip, to get him up and light, lets you shorten, but you have snuffed out the impulsion, so now you can't lengthen.

Neither balance nor impulsion, by itself, is good enough. You have to have both at the same time in the same canter, and not many riders have the exquisite feel to have their body worthy of being called a "tuning fork for the right canter." And it will be in the flatwork that these skills get honed, not over fences alone, because the horse simply cannot handle being over-jumped.

I heard Jack Le Goff say, so many times, "The link between impulsion and balance is the correct use of the half-halt."

So, here is a mission for the highly motivated rider. Become a tuning fork for that highly elusive adjustable canter, and this will serve you equally well if the objective is to do straight dressage, be a show jumping rider, or an event rider.

Creating the Right Show-Jumping Canter

The root cause of so much that goes wrong in jumping is the bad takeoff distance, especially from a bad canter. When the horse gets to a good distance from a good canter, then it is up to the horse to actually jump. The rider has basically done his or her job. And, generally speaking, by and large, that "good" distance is around 6 feet in front, and a "good" canter, as I mentioned already, is one that combines enough impulsion with enough balance.

Remember those three options when a horse gets too close?

1. Refuse.

2. Try to jump but crash it.

3. Do that helicopter jump, straight up, straight down.

When a horse gets too long, there are two options:

1. Leave with a flat launch.

2. Chip in another stride. When this happens, it is the same as if the horse got in too close to begin with.

Now, most top riders are different from all the not-so-good jumping riders, in that most of them do not get their horse time and again to a bad distance that makes their horse have to struggle. And most top riders have good eyes for distances partly because most top riders can create an adjustable canter that is like an accordion, in that the horse can shorten to avoid getting too close or lengthen to avoid getting too long. For this good canter to be installed, the horse must be strong enough behind to be capable of engaging his hocks under his body in a "spring-loading" action, so that he can rock back and jump up, not merely jump "at" the fence.

Most top riders can create an adjustable canter that is like an accordion, in that the horse can shorten to avoid getting too close or lengthen to avoid getting too long.

■ ■ ■

Want to become a better rider of jumpers? Become better at feeling the difference between just any old canter and an adjustable canter, which combines enough impulsion to let you move up, but at the same time contains enough balance to let you shorten. This skill opens the door to the acquisition of a good eye. A good eye helps the horse dramatically, because it can help the horse jump out of the optimum spot time after time.

If you can't do these two things very well, that is, create an adjustable canter or see a takeoff spot, you are a member of a big club. But then, most riders are not obsessed with honing skills through endless practice.

Engagement: In for a Penny, in for a Pound—or Not at All

Engagement, and not the kind with the diamond ring, is one of the great mysteries of the riding world. Maybe not for you, but it sure was for me.

The definition of engagement that I use is one I was told in Germany: "Engagement is the act of flexing the hocks, stepping with the hind legs under the body, planting the hooves on the ground, and lifting."

We see that horses can do this in nature. Take a horse out of the barn to his paddock on a crisp morning and turn him loose. Head up, tail up, he will float along in a gravity-defying trot, each step almost levitating him above the earth, boing, boing, boing, his highly engaged hocks and hind legs providing the lift with each stride. As soon as he gets tired, he stops the game and goes back to his normal way of moving, where the hocks propel him along and forward, but no longer provide much in the way of lift.

To have a horse that is truly light in front is to have that lightness made available as "lifted lightness," the byproduct of correctly engaged hocks. This is the opposite of the false illusion of lightness a horse gives when he is backing off discomfort in his mouth because of rough hands or a sharp bit or, most likely, a combination of both at once.

It took me forever to grasp the physics of this concept, but the creation of true engagement is a bedrock principle of classical riding, and without it, back-to-front riding inevitably becomes incorrect front-to-back riding.

Most riders ride front-to-back. When they want to slow down or stop, they pull on the reins. If the horse doesn't comply, they pull harder. If the horse still doesn't respond, they get a stronger bit, or they use draw reins or some other device to force the horse to submit to the backward pressure. Very few riders understand classical training methods enough to create lightness in front as a byproduct of strength behind. And from a purely practical standpoint, most riders can ride all their lives kicking to go and pulling to whoa and be perfectly fine and happy and successful. And once the horses begin to understand that backward mouth pressure means slow down, and they learn to give in to that pressure, the horses are likewise good to go. Unless the horse is nervous, or the rider is brutally rough, neither horse nor rider cares much that what is being done isn't considered classical from the purist point of view.

But just say that you do want to know more, so what's to figure out? Well, we already know that horses can lift into lightness because we've watched them do it on those frosty mornings, snorting and blowing in their paddocks. They lift by engaging, which is simply a different way of describing weightlifting. The weight the horse lifts is primarily his own weight, plus the added 15 to 20 percent that is the weight of his rider.

But how do we get a horse to step under his body with his hind legs, especially because getting him to do it causes athletically induced discomfort? As you will know if you've ever done it, weightlifting hurts. It makes your muscles ache and your heart beat faster, and it can make you gasp with effort. The human will put up with the discomfort of weightlifting because she wants to get stronger, but the horse could care less about getting stronger. All the horse thinks is how to avoid the stress by leaning on the bit, or by getting above or behind the bit, or by getting crooked in his body, or by speeding up or slowing down, anything that can prevent the rider from inducing him to engage his hocks under his body. He is not being "bad" by trying to avoid this. He simply is attempting to avoid the discomfort.

If we ask too little the horse doesn't get stronger. If we ask too much, he rebels.

■ ■ ■

So the rider is sitting on the horse, a leg on each side, usually carrying a dressage whip. We call the legs, and feet, and spurs, and whip the "driving aids."

The trick is to carefully push the horse into containment or restraint, thus coaxing those hind legs to reach under, where they will now have to lift as well as simply propel. And it is easier to do this one hind leg at a time because of the way a horse is built. Picture a horse going on a right-hand curve. We call the right side of the gently curved horse the "inside" and the left side the "outside." Our inside aids—right leg, seat bone, arm, wrist, hand—create a forward and outward pressure to the left. Our outside aids—left leg, arm, and so forth—"contain" the outward energy and redirect it to the right. These opposing forces, if we do it right, "induce" that inside hind leg (the right hind) to step more forward and more under the center of the horse's mass, so that each time that leg straightens, it lifts more weight. In terms of physics, we have "loaded" the inside hind leg. If that inside hind went that far, it would go between the front legs of the horse.

When we switch direction and curve the horse to the left, we switch all our aids so that now we are loading the left hind leg. Back and forth we go,

Speed Axcel

By the time I bought Speed Axcel, the hot little Thoroughbred mare that would be my last of 14 Advanced Level event horses, I had learned many of the riding skills that I hadn't possessed during the years of my more "public" competitive successes.

By that time, the mid- to late-1990s, I could quite reliably see my distances, so I was far less likely to get to bad take-off spots. I was pretty much able to create an adjustable canter, one that would give me a greater range of options about the distances that I could see. My jumping posture was pretty good, and I could look at the photos of myself jumping and not want to burn them.

But although I had finally learned, by my mid-fifties, basic skills that I wished I'd acquired decades sooner, I was still using antiquated and incorrect training methods. These were the ways of interacting with horses that I had first learned back in the rough-and-ready 1950s, articulated by phrases like, "Don't let him get away with that." "You've got to show him who's boss."

When I got Speed Axcel in my late fifties, I finally had to learn how to ride, because I–COULD–NOT–RIDE–HER in dressage.

And, "Make him mind."

When I bought Speed Axcel, I thought that in terms of jumping ability she was a reincarnation of Victor Dakin. She didn't so much "jump" over a fence as spring into the air—it was like the feeling of bounce you get from the end of a diving board, that extra kick and lift.

But as for dressage, Axcel was even more worried than Victor had been. I couldn't ride her calmly to save my soul. The slightest wrong move on my part would send her jigging sideways, or make her break into a canter, or switch leads, or career sideways. I couldn't ride her, and especially I couldn't ride her using any of the ways I had used for so long, based, if I am dead honest, on "making" the horse do some specific thing.

I know, in an intellectual sort of way, that horses are flight animals, quick to flee a predator rather than confront one. But in all the years prior to Axcel, I had never encountered a horse quite so sensitive to any hint of pressure or coercion. I had to either give up on Speed Axcel or make some fundamental changes in the way I trained a horse.

So there I was, 56 or 57 years old, having had all sorts of public success, realizing that I did not know how to train a difficult or worried horse. Not really. Not without using pressure or a degree of coercion, and neither worked with Axcel. I did not have the necessary "arrows in my quiver," and I knew it. What I did not know was how to fix it.

As I groped for answers that might help me unlock Axcel's worried mind, I somehow stumbled upon the German word *losgelassenheit*. That word was to

gradually lead to an epiphany in how I viewed the entire training process.

I can't give the exact translation from the German, and I don't want to get into one of those endless "dressage wars" over minutiae, but in general, here is how I understood the essence of *losgelassenheit*: We can think of a horse that is tight, and almost always a horse that is tight emotionally will be tight and stiff in his physical body. *Losgelassenheit* can be described as "a state of looseness," but that misses the point. I would rather think of it as meaning "an absence of tightness." And that means two kinds of tightness should not be present in a correct training process, neither physical tightness nor emotional tightness, also called emotional tension or anxiety.

I thought this through and came to some conclusions. What I had been taught so many years earlier, to think of a horse as something to be "made" to perform, inevitably necessitated enough pressure from the rider so that the horse would "obey" the demand. However, if that pressure from the rider was too intense or too extreme or too demanding, the horse might do what I was asking, but he would do

(continued)

Speed Axcel (continued)

it with the extremely negative byproduct of becoming nervous.

A little sidetrack here, but it will make sense as you see where it is going: As I've mentioned already, back in 280 BC King Pyrrhus of Epirus defeated the Romans in a couple of battles, but in doing so, his army suffered so many casualties that the next time he met the Romans, King Pyrrhus was crushed. Thus "Pyrrhic victory" came to mean a victory that exerts such a devastating toll on the victor that it is tantamount to defeat. I realized, after years and years of using too much pressure, that I had been winning too many Pyrrhic victories. By using aids that were too forceful, I had won the "battle" of, say, getting my horse to move off my leg, or jump a ditch, or whatever, but I had lost the "war," because I had

Two of my most talented jumpers were also two of my most difficult horses to ride in dressage. Here is Victor, teeth bared, blasting out of the 1977 Ledyard International starting gate, which was so typical of his attitude to life in general. It worked for cross-country, but not for dressage!

often created anxiety and tension and nervous fear in my horses. It was one of those gigantic light-bulb moments, the realization that I had too frequently been the root cause of my horse's resistance, and that the resistance my horses showed was embedded in the very methods that I had been using to persuade them not to resist.

With this newfound knowledge to guide me, I would go into the indoor ring, shut the door, so as to create a "library" atmosphere of quiet calm, and simply walk Axcel, trying to get her to release the tension that pervaded all her body parts: jaw, poll, hips, back, shoulders, neck. Basically, what I was trying (imperfectly, but trying) to do was to "say" to Axcel, "I know you are scared. I know you have no trust. I am not going to force you. I am not going to hurt you. I am trying not to scare you."

To some extent, it worked. I was pretty inexperienced, even as I neared age 60, in employing new ways, and Axcel had already been badly scarred by being pushed too hard at too young an age. But it marked the beginning of my feeling that I had finally made a real breakthrough in my ability to train.

In Retrospect: What I'd Do Differently with Speed Axcel

Speed Axcel's dressage issues were like Victor Dakin's dressage issues on steroids. To say that she was nervous about flatwork would be akin to assuming that Daniel had a twitch of anxiety when he found himself cast into a den of hungry lions.

I could – not – ride – her.

Of all the horses I have ever ridden, Speed Axcel was the one horse that most effectively taught me that all those precepts that I'd learned as a young kid back in western Massachusetts in the 1950s simply did not apply. And so, after decades of my resorting to creating pressure to deal with pressure, Axcel was the horse that was most responsible for creating a paradigm shift in my approach to training horses.

Ironically, Speed Axcel would be the last horse that I would ride at the Advanced Level of eventing, in June of 1999, at Groton House, a couple of months before my 58th birthday.

As they say, though, "Better late than never."

engaging first one and then the other hock, so that the horse is weightlifting primarily one hind leg at a time, depending on the direction he is turning.

It's tricky. If we ask too little the horse doesn't get stronger. If we ask too much, he rebels. A phrase I like is, "negotiated driving aids into negotiated restraining aids."

Week by week, little by little, month by month, the horse gets progressively stronger and more capable of lifting from behind. It is a slow and tedious process. No wonder so many riders just slap in a stronger bit and ride front-to-back. It's faster, simpler, and avoids all that work. Unfortunately, it doesn't lead to success.

And another thing: there's nothing wrong at all with riding on a loose rein, not asking for engagement at all. Many riding sports, like competitive trail riding, don't require a horse to sit and lift. So unless you're committed to the body-building process of consistent engagement, it might be better not to ask for engagement at all, because to do so sporadically means that the horse is never ready to do it. It will cause distress, he will resist, and this can lead to confrontation. That's why I chose the heading, "In for a Penny, in for a Pound." Do it or don't do it, but if you do it, don't just do it now and then and expect good results.

How to "Make" an Upper-Level Event Horse

If you have watched the Kentucky Three-Day Event, you may have been struck by how impossibly daunting it looks, especially the cross-country day. And, to be real, it *is* pretty daunting, even for those competitors who are used to riding at that level.

But at one time each of those riders was a little kid, and every one of those horses was a green baby, so they didn't just get tapped with some magic wand to suddenly arrive in Kentucky. They went through a process. If you can understand the process, then you can use it to either create your own four-star horse—or create a horse to the level that makes you happy.

The process that I'm going to describe has worked for me with lots of horses, including one that I bred and raised from a foal (fig. 3.8). Do I think my way is the only way? Absolutely not. There are "many roads to Rome." But because it is a path that I know and understand, it is a path that I can describe. Part of what follows is described in generalities. If I say, "Do this when the horse is age four," he might be three, or five, or even older. These are guide-

3.8: An upper-level event horse, like Victor Dakin here, is born with potential, but then that potential is tapped and created through proper training. Genetics can't do it alone. Neither can training. We need both. Victor and I are in the middle of our show-jumping round at the World Championships at Burghley, England, in 1974, in this photograph.

lines rather than rules fixed in stone, and should be used or discarded, as it seems best in some particular circumstance.

But, keeping in mind the saying, "Fools rush in where angels fear to tread," here is how it might work for you and your horse:

Four years old—maybe he already has raced. Maybe he got started at age three under saddle and is used to hacking out on trails. Maybe he is green as grass. Whatever. A four-year-old horse is a place to start.

So I want to be able to get on him and ride him without being bucked off and hurt. There are other books about getting the total green bean to the, "I can now ride him" stage, so read those books, or get help. We will assume that this four-year-old can be ridden with reasonable safety.

The first thing I do—once I know he basically goes, stops, and turns right and left, and is likely to do all that without suddenly turning into a terrorist— is to start him going on walks with an older, wiser, calmer friend. I want the relaxed attitude of the buddy horse to reassure my baby that he is safe and doesn't need to stop and not go forward, or to spook or whirl or spin. I just want him to walk quietly while he gets used to life. If he is an off-the-track Thoroughbred, he will have already experienced life, some of it better, some of it worse.

In any case, he needs to get used to terrain, uphill, downhill, and he needs to get used to footing, dry, wet, muddy, rough, even rocky. He needs to go through puddles and small streams, and he needs to get comfortable with becoming an "outdoor" horse. As we've discussed, some riders have access to amazing trail systems, but some don't. If you don't, this will be harder to do, all the walking part.

As he walks, four or five days each week, 45 minutes to an hour and 15 minutes a day, he will start getting stronger and much more fit. It is easy to make the mistake of thinking, "I am only walking." If you are actively kicking along, not strolling or ambling, you are probably doing about 3.5 to 4 miles an hour. You can turn an unfit horse into a well-muscled athlete if you have him in a consistent walking program. You are quietly creating a topline, plus you are hardening all those systems I've mentioned—his heart, lungs, tendons, ligaments, muscles, hooves, and bones. Never think the walk is an irrelevant gait, or that time spent walking is time wasted. A good walk can be your secret weapon.

Now it has been four, five, maybe six months. You have a four-year-old who is used to being caught every day, groomed, tacked up, and ridden. You have a horse that is starting to be a riding horse. You haven't hurt him, and with luck, you haven't had many fights about things, so you haven't scared him. He's fit, used to someone sitting on him, and ready to start to learn some basics.

The Basics

Basics, basics, basics, the often ignored, often misunderstood, often underutilized building blocks by which the untrained horse is slowly turned into a trained one.

Think of your green four-year-old as that mostly "unprogrammed computer" we talked about on page 79. You are the program installer. Your job is to turn this young horse into a programmed computer, and you are going to do this in ways that do not scare him, hurt him, or force him.

What are some early basics? Well, many of these have been already installed by your months of quiet walking. He already understands go and stop, turn right, turn left, stand still, so you are way ahead of the game. Remember, aids are nonverbal communications. We use pressure and release instead of spoken words. He already understands the leg or tapping stick to go forward, rein pressure to slow down or stop, right rein to turn right, left rein to turn left, so you and he are already "talking" to one another. Now you will add leg pressure to your rein pressure (fig. 3.9). As you circle left, you ask him to move away from your left calf out into your right hand, and the opposite when you circle right. Accept

> Never think the walk is an irrelevant gait, or that time spent walking is time wasted. A good walk can be your secret weapon.
>
> ■ ■ ■

3.9: "Lateral" means sideways. Horses move sideways on their own, for all sorts of reasons. We take that innate ability, and hone and shape it through training. Lateral work, as Carrie Ramsey is doing here with Beaulieu's Cool Concorde (Cordi), increases flexibility and suppleness.

the fact that he will be too weak about engaging his hind end, and reticent about having a steady contact on the bit. Don't ask for very much for very long. He's four, just a baby. Don't get greedy. Don't think because your friend Terry is already jumping her four-year-old that you are behind in your training process. Remember, this little guy is maybe headed to the Kentucky Three-Day. We are not going to mess up long-term goals for short-term gratification.

You will have done some trotting out on the trails with his buddy horse, but now you start more trotting in the ring. He will speed up, slow down, lose his balance, fuss with his head position, now above the bit, now behind the bit. Stay cool, no big deal. He's just weak and green. He is not being "resistant." He is not being "bad." He just doesn't get it, and even if he did, he isn't strong enough to sustain it.

Head Setting: A Flawed Concept

Don't try to "set" your horse's head. He'll put his head where he needs it to be a sort of balancing rudder. Later, he'll put his head into a more "orthodox" position, but don't get into it with him because he's all over the place with his head position. Sure, he shouldn't root and yank you out of the saddle, or fling his head and break your nose. If he does that stuff, something else may be wrong. But we'll assume he has no glaring problems.

Now at some point, you have to canter this baby. If he's a former racehorse, he's done lots of cantering and galloping, but he probably doesn't know his right and left lead signals, and he may associate cantering with bolting off into the next county. So be careful. Horses tend to learn their lead signals out of a trot on a circle. Go right at a trot, put your left leg behind the girth, cluck, and see what happens. He may just trot faster. He may kick out. He may get the lead you want. He may get the wrong lead.

If he gets it, go along with him for a little bit, and then return to the trot. If he messes up, and this is more normal, just come back to the trot and try again. Some of them get it faster than others. Try not to get too intense or too frustrated if he seems to be a slow learner. He'll get it, but he'll get it sooner if you don't panic or get mad at him. It may take several weeks, though, even a few months, before he's any kind of reliable about picking up his correct canter leads.

So now you have been riding this four-year-old for six or seven or eight months. He walks, trots, and canters. He (sort of) goes, stops, steers right and left. He crosses streams, climbs hills, goes through mud, and picks his way through bad footing.

Le Goff's Advice

Here's how the two words, "He ought" and the three words, "He knows better" run counter to Jack Le Goff's advice on how to train horses:

Le Goff said, "Boldness comes from confidence. Confidence comes from success. So it is the mission of the trainer to create lots of situations that as much as possible guarantee success."

Here, though, I think, we should realize that Le Goff was not only talking about jumping. While it applies very well to jumping, it applies equally to almost everything that creates anxiety or tension or a lack of comprehension in a horse.

As an example, someone takes a horse out trail riding alone. The horse would be calmer and steadier if he had company, especially quiet company, but the rider says, "He ought to be able to handle this on his own." Or a horse moves around at the mounting block, and the rider says, as she yanks him around, "He knows better." Or loading into a trailer. Or standing while tied. Or being quiet for the farrier. Or accepting being clipped.

A horse does not "fake" being anxious in order to "get out of work" or because "he is being bad."

Sure, the horse does need to learn how to load, to stand still while being shod, to not move off while being

Meet In Khartoum and Portada give encouragement to one another.

mounted, to handle being ridden alone, but if he doesn't understand these things, or if they scare him or make him nervous, Jack Le Goff's advice is to start by creating little successes, rather than to get into battles to "make him settle down."

The only way you can "make" a horse be calm is by drugging him. You can longe or gallop to exhaustion, and he will be quiet, perhaps, but underneath the tiredness will still be nervousness.

So what is so wrong with trail riding with a buddy at first, or doing tons of quiet transitions with a mild bit rather than by cranking him into a harsh bit, if it makes him calmer? Or by giving him a lead through water or over a small ditch, instead of whaling on him to make him go because, "He ought to go because he knows better?" Or any kind of strategy to build confidence by success rather than to force obedience through things that hurt or scare him?

And, yes, I do agree that there are times where "he ought to know better." When a horse pins his ears and threatens you when you are graining

A horse needs to be confident about going into the trailer.

him, or crowds you in the wash stall, or cow kicks at you while you are grooming, or similar behaviors, sure, he may need to be "taught a lesson." But generally, "teaching him a lesson" should not be the normal "go-to" method if the goal is to build lasting confidence.

Or maybe Le Goff is the one who didn't "get" how to train horses? Maybe we are smarter horse people than Jack Le Goff?

Sure. Dream on....

Maybe it's time to introduce some jumping. "Jumping" may be too gran-
diose a term for what I have in mind. My goal for this baby is to create a conditioned response mechanism so that when he sees something in front of him
he simply "knows" that it is his job to get to the other side, and to do it calmly.

I do this by making his first exposure to "jumping" so ridiculously easy
that he can literally step over the tiny jumps (fig. 3.10). I am aiming for a "no
big deal" response: see it, trot up to it, and either step over it or jump over
it—up to him. I will do this time and again, maybe two or three times a week,
10 or 15 tiny jumps, until I have the sense that he can do it in his sleep. Only

3.10: "Make the task so simple they can't fail to achieve it. If that doesn't work, make
it easier." Meet In Khartoum's first ever attempt at "jumping," with Kendall Szumilas.

then will I raise the jumps so that they are actual jumps rather than just step-over cross-rails or tiny verticals.

The whole point of this goes back to that famous Jack Le Goff mantra that I talk about in the sidebar on page 126.

It is so simple: Let him get confident by keeping it simple. Then, once that confidence about jumping is installed, make the jumps harder, or higher, wider, whatever. But not until you have created that "see it, jump it" conditioned response. I try to do this with both show jumps and cross-country obstacles, but this is only possible when I have access to tiny cross-country jumps, because these can't be lowered or raised the way we can lower or raise jumps with standards and rails in cups.

If I've done all of this well, our four-year-old will end the year with lots of installed basics, and he won't have been pounded on or pressured. He should be sound, sane, and confidently ready for his five-year-old season, which includes competing at the Beginner Novice Level. It may also involve competing at the Novice Level, if the Beginner Novice experience is positive.

A Look Ahead

Just to take a look down the road, if all goes well, think, "Where will he be, and when should he be there?"

This is not fixed in stone by any means, but here is a possible long-term scenario for the talented horse trained by a talented rider.

Age 4: Basic walk-trot-canter, begin baby jumping.

Age 5: Beginner Novice and Novice events, five to seven of these (fig. 3.11).

Age 6: Novice Level half the season, Training Level second half.

Age 7: Training Level until the horse feels confident enough to go Preliminary.

Age 8: Preliminary. Maybe, late season, move up to Intermediate.

3.11: Start with easy tasks to make the horse feel like he is king of the world. Core Buff became an advanced event horse, but he gained the confidence to do so by being asked simple tasks when he was young and green. Here, he is jumping tiny tires at four years old.

Age 9: Preliminary or Intermediate, perhaps go up, go down, go back up.

Age 10: Intermediate, and, if all the ability and confidence is there, the big move up to Advanced.

Age 11: Advanced.

Age 12: Three Star.

Age 13: Four Star: Kentucky or Badminton or Burghley.

Some horses will never get this far. Some horses will do it one or two, even three years sooner. Much depends upon the horse and the skill and experience of the rider. My scenario is both conservative and optimistic. Optimistic that this is an actual four-star horse, conservative in giving him nine years to get there after his four-year-old start.

So many pieces of the big puzzle are still out in the unknown future of the four-coming-five-year-old. The dressage challenges, year by year, level by level. The cross-country "questions" that become both bigger and increasingly complex: corners, ditches, drops, water, angles, skinnies, all the things a course designer can create to challenge the horses and riders. And then, after galloping boldly on cross-country, can the horse leave the rails in the show-jumping cups?

There is a biblical statement, "Many are called, but few are chosen," that applies to riders and horses who aspire to the highest levels in any riding sport. In eventing, I think there might at any time, in all of North America, be 25,000 riders who event at some level, "minnow" to four star. There may be 50 who could possibly get around a four-star event, which means that for every 500 event riders, one might be a four-star rider. That is one-fifth of one percent, long odds against, but when did long odds ever stop a dreamer? Look at this another way: Somebody will be one of those 50. Why not you?

And the same long odds against apply to the horses that carry those 50 riders, and it is because of that the prices of elite horses have skyrocketed in the past 10 years or so, to the point that a million-dollar event horse is no longer unthinkable.

So if you dream big, get a nice young horse and begin the steady process. In any case, you will learn how to train, so that if this horse isn't the chosen one, you will be better prepared to try again. Somebody is going to make those superstar horses. Why shouldn't it be you?

Keys to the Kingdom

"Keys to the Kingdom": Do they actually exist or is it not that simple? This is a phrase that I have always taken to mean as "things" that, if we somehow possess them, will unlock the doors to those magical places to which we aspire to go.

The last book I wrote is called *How Good Riders Get Good;* it explores the paths and strategies used by a number of high achievers, and if that's your thing, read the book.

In "real life," I suspect that most riders want to feel fulfilled and happy, riding nice horses, at levels that match their comfort zone and their competence level. They are not interested in high drama, white-knuckled anxiety, or any sort of adversarial relationship with a horse. Most riders want to enjoy their riding, and most riders want their horses to enjoy being ridden. I am convinced that most of us who ride are committed to the welfare of the horses that take us where we want to go.

So what is one transcendently important "key to the kingdom?" Empathy. The ability to put ourselves in our horse's shoes, and to be able to feel what our horse wants and needs.

There was a cartoon in a book of stories about Vermont edited by Keith Warren called *Green Mountains and Rock Ribs.* It showed a little boy holding a horse. An old man asks, "So, sonny, how did you find that lost horse everyone's been hunting for?" The little boy replies, "I thought, if I was a horse, where would I go, and I did, and he had."

We have to be like that little boy. We have to think, "If I was a horse," what would I want? And then, within reason, provide it. If we can think like that, and act like that, I think we can rightly claim to be good horse people. And what could be better than that?

Right Training Overcomes Wrong Instinct

Many riding faults are instinct driven. Humans are eye-hand oriented. Think of the thousand-and-one things we do every day where our eyes direct our hands to perform a task. Now we're on a horse, and to some extent we use our hands to position his head. So what do we do? We look down to see what's going on down there. The classic "ear, shoulder, hip, heel of inside foot" straight line has been broken, because as the eyes look down, it's like dominos. The eyes look down, the head tips forward, the shoulders round, the upper body inclines, and, instead of looking like Isabell Werth, the rider looks like Quasimodo.

Or what's the instinct-driven thing riders do so often to "help" the horse jump? They lean. In running, when you want to go faster, you lean. Same for skating, riding a bike. Why shouldn't it work for jumping? But then you see all the photos of the praying mantis look, the rider halfway up the horse's neck, her heels back by the horse's hips.

What happens, instinctively, when a rider gets nervous? The rider tightens. Theoretically, the rider needs to stay *more* supple and elastic, to help the horse remain supple and elastic, but when instinct rules, the opposite happens.

> For people who are motivated and disciplined enough to accept it, correct, systematic training will overcome wrong instinct.
>
> ■ ■ ■

General Sid Shachnow, my friend and Southern Pines, North Carolina, neighbor, was formerly in command of all US Special Forces, men who are incredibly well trained to perform under the highest pressures. Sid told me that the most instinctive reaction soldiers have when suddenly ambushed is to turn and run away, which greatly lessens their chances of survival. Sid went on to explain that his men were trained, instead, to run directly at the ambushing force, firing their weapons.

Sid's point: if soldiers can be trained to run into live rifle fire, then it follows logically that riders can be trained to look up, and to not jump ahead of the motion. For people who are motivated and disciplined enough to accept it, correct, systematic training will overcome wrong instinct.

"Fatigue Makes Cowards of Us All." —Vince Lombardi

So you have this horse and you want to train it. The very first thing to consider, and the big piece of the puzzle, which many otherwise good riders and trainers so often miss, is to truly evaluate how fit or unfit the horse actually is.

A fit horse can withstand work that will fling an unfit horse into instant distress. The distressed horse will, in despair, resist. The resistance will cause many a rider to conclude that the horse is being bad/naughty/disobedient and will add to the already distress-causing pressure. The horse is screwed. And the rider did it to the horse. And nothing good can come of it. And the rider blames the horse.

Think about this the next time you start to get into it with a horse. Of the many bad/stupid/ignorant mistakes I made with horses, this is one of the worst. Get the horse fit first, and *then* ask more. Do not do it the wrong way around.

Leadership Insights
from Two US Army Generals and a US Navy Admiral

When I was in my teens, our summer next-door neighbors in South Reading, Vermont, were Vice Admiral Joel Boone, and his wife, Helen. Admiral Boone was a frequent visitor at our house, as he and my father would spend long hours driving Dad's Morgan, Millers Commander.

Admiral Boone was the most highly decorated medical officer in the history of the US Armed Services: a World War I recipient of the Congressional Medal of Honor and six silver stars. Yet in all my many visits with him, the thing that I noticed most was his quiet, self-deprecatory manner. His leadership qualities were simply "there," with no need for pretension.

I took riding lessons from Major General Jack Burton, a former Olympic Three-Day rider, who had an extremely systematic way of training. Jack would say, "In the Army, we tell them what we are going to tell them. Then we tell them. Then we tell them what we told them." Yes, it is repetitive, but yes, it is effective.

You've read the advice that Major General Sid Shachnow gave me when I complained to him about how difficult it was to teach riders not to jump "ahead of the motion" over fences (see p. 133). "Denny," Sid said, "if I can train my guys to run into live rifle fire, you can teach your riders not to jump up the neck. Training has to overcome instinct."

"On No Given Day..."

If I had to choose just one mistake, one misconception that plagued me more than any other in my years of training and riding horses, it would be that I didn't understand this one simple truth:

On no given day, in no given training session, are we going to accomplish very much with a horse.

Think of yourself. If you went to work out at a gym with a personal trainer, would you expect to be transformed after one session? Would you have

A: Vice Admiral Joel Boone and Mrs. Boone.
B: Major General Jonathan Burton.
C: Left to right: Major General Sid Shachnow, me, Arlene Shachnow, and their daughter Denise Smith.

become an overnight sensation? Would you have mastered some new skill? "No way," you would say. "That's not how it works. It takes months of training and practice to make any sort of substantial difference."

And yet, even knowing this, how easy it is to get into an endless drill with some poor horse. "Do it again. No, that's not good enough. Do it again."

The horse gets tired, scared, more resistant. The rider gets frustrated, annoyed, more insistent. A perfect recipe for an unproductive schooling session. So here is what it has taken me far too many years to fully appreciate: Forward progress is much slower than backward deterioration.

It takes a long time to make a horse, but we can wreck a horse in no time at all. And it takes far less skill. Heck, anybody can wreck a horse.

Like the Cards in the Deck

One good way to visualize this truth is the deck of playing cards analogy (fig. 3.12). There are 52 cards in a deck, just as there are 52 weeks in a year. So think of a single card as representing one week of work with a horse. Lay

that card on a table. It doesn't make a very high stack, does it? You can scarcely see it, looked at from the side.

Now put down 10 cards, representing 10 weeks of work with a horse. Slightly more visible, but hardly a significant stack. And remember, each card represents an entire week of work with a horse.

The point is, why the big rush? Neither horses nor humans improve much by quantum leaps, but by gradual progression. However, you can create quantum leaps of deterioration by fighting with a horse, or by pushing a horse so hard that

3.12: One card, five, even 10, hardly seem like anything, but stacked up, one atop another, they create something visible and substantial. So it is with training horses, one day, one week, one month, one year at a time.

he becomes sore, sour, and resentful. So take it easy, session by session. Get a little, think, "Hey, this is pretty good," and quit for the day. Go for a nice hack in the woods. Try a little more tomorrow. Stack those cards.

Sooner than you think, you will find some sweet day that things your horse didn't used to be able to do, he now knows how to do. "When did that happen?" you will ask.

Well, it was happening all along, but you were too close to it to see the changes. It is like looking at your face every day in the mirror. You look the same today as yesterday. Tomorrow you will look the same as today.

> Neither horses nor humans improve much by quantum leaps, but by gradual progression.
>
> ◼ ◼ ◼

But if you see a photo of yourself from some years ago, you look different. When did you change? You were changing all along, like the horse, but you were too close to it to notice that it was happening.

Give the horse a chance. Work a little. Ask a little. Get a little. Say thank you and go do something else. Of the many tricks of the horse-training trade that I wish I had learned decades sooner, this is at the top of my list.

"Lying to a Horse"

Years ago, when Rodney Jenkins was the leading American show jumping rider, there was an article about him that asked a question about training a horse to jump. The question was why some horses seem to progress more rapidly than others. "Is it raw talent? Is it training? What is it that gives a horse confidence?"

Then the article referred to a number of the (admittedly talented) jumpers that Rodney had produced, and postulated that one of the main reasons that they had progressed up the levels so rapidly had to do with the fact that Rodney "had never lied to them."

The author of the article explained that one of the worst ways to "lie" to a green jumper was to repeatedly get him to take off from places in front of a

Farnley Rob Roy

Farnley Rob Roy was bred by the same Virginia farm that produced the Farnley Welsh ponies. He was a big, raw-boned gray, out of a Canadian draft hunt mare, and he got his phenomenal jumping ability from his sire, New Twist, a son of the immortal Bonne Nuit. New Twist also sired six-time show jumping Olympian Frank Chapot's jumper stallion Good Twist, who sired the Olympic silver medal jumper Gem Twist. The Twist family could jump, and Robbie could jump, and more importantly, would jump just about any cross-country fence I aimed him at.

After I figured out how to ride him, I competed at four of the biggest American three-day events, twice at Chesterland, Pennsylvania, and twice at the Kentucky Three-Day, and he never had a single jumping fault in either cross-country or show jumping.

Rob Roy was not fancy, and his trot was far from being that springy, floating gait that makes dressage judges weak in the knees and wanting to dole out eights and nines. He wasn't an easy

Farnley Rob Roy was not the most supremely gifted horse I ever rode, but he had huge scope, and he was as game as they come.

galloper, either, but he was what Nor-man Hall used to call "Game as Tracy." (Dick Tracy was a comic strip cop who would be shot full of holes, but would just keep coming.)

Robbie was the only horse that I rode for any length of time that we didn't actually own. Matthew and Winkie Mackay-Smith let me have the ride after the woman who took him to Intermediate no longer had the time to take from her busy veterinary prac-tice, and when he came to me, he came with a big fat snaffle bit as his stan-dard equipment.

Now, if you listen to the bitting purists, they may tell you that all horses that are properly trained and ridden should be able to perform cor-rectly in a big fat snaffle, but from my experience, that is a big fat hoax.

I'd come thundering down on Rob-bie toward some vertical cross-country jump, when the last thing I'd want was for him to be on his forehand, and I would sit up and take a half-halt on that big fat snaffle. I might as well have tried to stop a Union Pacific freight train with a piece of thread. I would have to start getting him up so far in front of the jump to have any prayer of getting him "spring-loaded" back

on his hocks that I was racking up all kinds of time penalties, which would kill my score even if I jumped around clean.

I knew that Bill Steinkraus used a type of bit called a Tom Thumb Pelham on some of his jumpers, and I figured that if the best jumper rider in the world used one, he must have had his reasons, and if it was good enough for Steinkraus, it would be more than good enough for me.

The term "Tom Thumb" refers to the short shanks on the Pelham bit. (The original Tom Thumb was a little person who performed in the Barnum and Bailey circus, hence the name.) Anyway, I put one of those on Robbie's big gray head, and it was an instant miracle cure. I would sit up, take a tug, and Robbie would sit down and lift up like a Harrier jet. You learn something from every horse you ride if you are tuned in to learning, and learning to ignore pontificating from armchair bit experts was one thing I learned from riding Rob Roy.

Speaking of Steinkraus, he once wrote a caption in one of his books—next to a photo of him riding Ksar D'Esprit over a 7-foot wall—that if his

(continued)

Farnley Rob Roy (continued)

life depended on clearing one of them, he would want to be sitting on that horse.

If my life depended on going clear around the hardest cross-country course, Farnley Rob Roy would be the horse I would want to ride. Robbie wasn't the fanciest horse I ever rode, or the fastest, or the most beautiful, but he was sound and tough and brave and bold, and I could have jumped him through a flaming hoop.

In Retrospect: What I'd Do Differently with Farnley Rob Roy

The shape of a horse's topline can be changed by certain kinds of riding. The crest can be developed, the connection over the loins strengthened if the horse can be induced to work "over the back." Robbie was not an orthodox shape for a dressage horse. He was a bit high in the hips compared to his withers, and his neck was set on somewhat low. Despite that, Robbie could jump a small building, but the thing that kept him from being top of the line in the former long-format, three-day sport was his dressage. He wasn't hot or nervous;

There is no "one size fits all" type of bit. This Tom Thumb Pelham works wonders on some I've ridden, but failed utterly to improve the performance of others.

he just didn't look the part.

The connection, back-to-front "circle of energy," I now think, looking back 35 years, is something that could have been improved. How much, or how dramatically improved, I don't know.

But that is the one big thing that I would work on if I could do it all again.

3.13: Even on green beans like future Olympic medal winner HO Sloopy here, Rodney gave his horses enormous freedom and confidence, because "he never lied to them."

fence from which it was either very difficult or impossible to leave the ground without smashing through it (fig. 3.13). In other words, many riders, less talented than Rodney, might come cantering toward a jump and arrive, let's say, 8 feet in front of the jump instead of the more desirable 6 feet. This is known as "seeing a long spot," and we talked about the choices (all of them bad) it gives the horse back on page 112.

In all cases, the rider has "lied" to the horse, because the rider has got the horse to a takeoff point that the horse either finds is impossible to jump from or, at least, difficult to jump from. And a horse that is constantly being lied to will become increasingly insecure, and may even turn into a "quitter," the term used to describe a horse who frequently refuses to jump.

Rodney Jenkins, by contrast, virtually never missed his distance. He gave his horses great security and confidence by making their jobs as easy as possible. Rodney's horses were helped by his great riding skills to achieve lots of success, and so their confidence grew, and those horses became bold horses.

The Art of Following: Lead Them, Because They Are Used to Being Led

"But Ruth said, 'Do not urge me to leave you or to return from following you. For where you go I will go.'"

Although this quotation is from the Bible, it applies to training horses in many cases, whether on foot or on another horse.

Recently I took Meet In Khartoum on a longe line down by the bank and little ditch below our jump ring. I walked up the ramp onto the bank, stepped off the other side, and Khartoum plopped off behind me. Then she hopped up, following me onto the bank.

So then I led her up to the ditch. She stopped, looking at it with suspicion. After a couple of minutes, I led her around to the other side, and she stopped again, but this time got close enough to sniff down at the edge and really check out the ditch.

So I led her away, and walked back, walked over it without looking at Khartoum, and she followed me. I gave her a peppermint, and walked back from the new side, and again she followed. I gave her another peppermint.

Then I set up a tiny jump, a standard on one side and a small plastic box on the other side, and let her trot over that from both directions.

Then, at the end, I took her back to the ditch, where she followed me back and forth one last time before I put her back in her field.

4

A Rider's Emotional Makeup and Character Traits

The Predator Within

Think of a list of opposites that someone might choose from in an attempt to describe what another person is like. Kind versus cruel. Optimistic versus pessimistic. Brave versus timid. Gentle versus rough. Patient versus impatient. Serious versus shallow. Reliable versus unreliable. There are dozens of others.

Now consider a human as he or she is trying to relate to a horse. As a species, a horse is known as a "prey animal," a creature that will flee danger, given the choice, rather than address danger. Here I do not mean the way stallions fight for herd dominance or breeding rights, because even rabbits will attack each other over these matters. A prey animal will flee from predator species that the prey species has reason to fear. A horse won't flee a hunting domestic cat, but he will try to escape from a hunting mountain lion.

Many humans have character traits that turn them into predators, at least insofar as a horse sees or senses the situation. Rough, loud, adversarial, impatient, determined humans are about as custom-made to create fear and distress in a horse as a hunting pack of wolves. The horse fears what he perceives as a threat to his safety, and plenty of riders come equipped with emotions and character traits guaranteed to threaten and scare horses.

When a good rider applies an aid, that rider does not "mumble."

■ ■ ■

Sometimes it isn't clear whether some interaction with horses should go under the heading of "horse training" or under "character traits," because there is often considerable overlap.

Say we have a rider, a highly driven, highly competitive perfectionist, who's schooling a horse. The poor horse can't seem to get the "perfect" canter depart, so the rider makes the horse do it again and again. This harmful training procedure is flowing directly from the basic makeup of the rider.

As you read through the examples on the following pages, try to consider the traits you have that you are happy to possess. And perhaps you'll find a few that you realize you might want to change. Be optimistic about this. Change is always possible, and it is never too late.

So You Want to Be a Horse Whisperer?

To become a "real" horse whisperer, don't be bamboozled by a lot of mystical mush about magical communication between horse and human (fig. 4.1). Horses don't "talk" with humans the way humans do with other humans. A rider doesn't use words to say to a horse, "Pick up the left lead canter by the letter B." As we discussed in chapter three, humans "talk" with horses through a system of constantly weaving and adjusting series of pressures and releases, each pressure or series of pressures, for a certain duration, at a certain intensity, upon a certain part of the horse's body, asking for a certain specific response from the horse.

4.1: Walt Gervais is probably not about to "whisper" to Timmy. "Horse whisperer" is more a figure of speech than a reality, despite all the hype that we read and hear.

Great riders who have ridden at the international level like George Morris and Frank Chapot in show jumping, and Klaus Balkenhol in dressage, will have a much larger and more expertly "spoken" vocabulary than the average kick-and-pull rider who can't sit the gaits and has little control over his or her lurching and bouncing body parts. When a good rider "applies an aid," which is simply horse speak for creating some specific pressure or series of pressures, to elicit some specific response that the horse has been trained to do, that rider does not "mumble." The aid is cleanly and clearly applied, and instantly softened, as a "reward," at the first hint of response by the horse, because good riders not only know the "language" but also are so totally in control of their own body that they are able to convey their requests in precise ways that the horse clearly understands.

I think if you ask the average rider, "What are aids?" many will not have a clear understanding that an aid is simply a nonverbal communication asked by the rider, not with a tongue and vocal cords but with a series of pressures and releases, each very specific, and always the same, each time.

When a human is sitting at the table and wants the salt, she does not ask for the ketchup. A good rider does not ask for a left lead canter by asking for a right lead canter, and so on.

Finding and Making the Time to Ride

Riding is a total passion for some, almost as necessary as breathing, and those people structure their lives to make certain that they can ride every day. I call these "hardcore" riders. We say that they would ride their horse by car head-light after work in a Minnesota blizzard. Nothing short of jail, crippling injury, or death is going to keep these riders away from saddle time (fig. 4.2). They will move to places that allow them to ride. They will take jobs that give them the time to ride. Because riding is such an absolute priority, they are often the ones who ride for a living, teach riding, or run boarding stables, and are the ones who do whatever it takes, even if that "whatever" includes giving up other parts of their life that most people might think of as necessities.

Down a notch on the "must ride" scale are what I think of as "three-quarter-core" riders. They may have as great a love of riding as their hard-core fellows, but something has gotten somewhat in the way. They may have

4.2: Want to be a good rider? Ride. In all conditions. Ride. Core Buff in the depths of a Vermont winter.

demanding jobs, demanding children, a demanding family situation, or some rigid economic necessity that prevents them from plunging full-bore into horses. They would like to be full-time riders, but something even more necessary has imposed itself between them and their saddle.

Now we get to the vast mass of riders I call "half-core" riders, those who, while they like to ride and are often quite good at it, can either take it or leave it, or have little choice but to take it or leave it. These include students with stringent time demands, parents of small children, commuters to distant jobs, military personnel, those who may have health issues, those financially challenged—there are so many reasons why many riders must accept this half-core status.

> The great challenge for most riders can be summed up easily in two words: time and money.
>
> ■ ■ ■

Now "soft-core" riders may actually own horses but rarely ride them. They may take the occasional lesson or be in a school or college riding program. These riders may go on trail rides with their friends who have that extra horse needing to be ridden. But whatever the situation, that passion to ride is just not there. These are the people who ride if and when it is convenient. They won't ride when it's cold. They won't ride when it's raining. They won't ride early, and they won't ride late. They can ride; they sort of like to ride. But if something better comes along, the horse can clearly wait.

The great challenge for most riders can be summed up easily in two words: time and money. And of the two, the big one is money, because if someone has enough money, this rider can buy the time. She can hire a babysitter; she can buy a farm. She can afford not to commute. She can buy horses. If she is rich enough, she can afford not to work at all.

So, because money, or the annoying lack of it, is such an impediment, I think it is worth thinking about strategies that allow not just the rich and famous to ride, but also the poor and obscure. Jack Le Goff used to say, "Because I was not born with the wealth I deserve, I have had to work for a living."

The Main Impediments to Riding More

So what are some of the biggest impediments to being able to ride more on a tight budget? I think there are four human impediments, and while you may actually love some of them, you may also find yourself in conflict with them.

These are dismissive spouses. Dismissive children. Dismissive parents. Dismissive employers. Dismissive how? Dismissive because they don't get your passion for horses, and because they don't get it, or share it, or sympathize with it, they tend to blow it off as something insignificant. And it *is* insignificant, to them, compared to the hundred-and-one other things in life that they consider more important. All of which can turn into an emotional minefield if you aren't careful. There is no easy answer; if there were one, there wouldn't be so much conflict.

Another impediment is the time taken up by your job. You need the job to pay for the horse, but the demands of the job prevent you from spending more time at the barn. Can you get a different job? Can you get a job that takes less of your time without affecting how much you make? Can you find either a place to work nearer the barn or a barn nearer the place you work? If you are one of the passionate riders, approaching that hardcore status, have you considered a job dealing with horses that also lets you ride? A note of caution here: I know several equine veterinarians who became equine vets because they loved to ride, but find that they are so busy that they almost never can ride. Not all horse jobs are riding jobs.

> You need the job to pay for the horse, but the demands of the job prevent you from spending more time at the barn.
>
> ■ ■ ■

If riding is lower on your list, but you simply crave more access to horses, there are lots of horse-related jobs that put you in contact with the whole riding scene.

Not long ago at our farm, a saddle rep for one of the big German saddlemakers spent half the day fitting saddles to a range of horses. So that's a job possibility. Tack shops, especially those with mobile units that go to shows, are another. Veterinary technicians who travel with vets, still another.

Equine dentists, massage therapists, farriers, van drivers, office workers at the big stallion farms, racetrack jobs—from hot walker to track management to bloodstock agents to auctioneers—wherever there are horses or horse products, there are horse-related jobs.

One person that I'm thinking of is the young (or middle-aged) professional with a pickup truck, a dog, a saddle, and a dream.

It is a tough way to live in many ways. No health insurance. No reliably steady source of income. No job security. Often no relationship. It's dangerous, riding lots of horses, and it's easy to get hurt. And yet, despite all odds, some of these wing-and-a-prayer riders break through and become some of those famous riders we read about in the magazines.

Others eventually give up the dream and settle into a safer, more "normal" job. And some will be okay with that, though others will regret it their whole lives through.

Overcoming Fear After Riding Accidents— and Fear of Riding in General

It's easy to be a brave rider if you are young and fit and athletic and you have never been hurt in a riding accident.

Horses, though, are big and quick, and you are up high when you are on top of one, and it is easy to get spun off, bucked off, lurched off, shied off—and, in every case, your body will slam into the ground, not unlike falling off a moving step ladder when you were on the highest step.

Most of the time, miraculously, we get up and walk away from falls, but that isn't always the case. I have a friend who is a logger by profession, and he told me that there is a saying among those who use chainsaws on a daily basis, "It isn't a question of whether you are going to get cut by a chainsaw. It's a question of when and how badly."

I think there are similar realities for riders. One saying is, "The only people who never fall off horses are the people who never get on horses." In other words, if you ride, you will fall off. And, just like the chainsaw quotation, since it isn't a question of *whether* we will fall off, it becomes a question of when and if we will get hurt as a result, and if so, how badly.

I do realize that some riders are comfortable with risk, and some are extremely risk averse. When the higher-risk "junkie" gets hurt, usually this rider will bounce back faster and with less residual baggage than the risk-averse rider whose fears have been realized. The degree of pain, the severity of the injury, the duration of the recovery—all these factor into the level of anxiety that remains after the fall.

I've known riders who've had horrific falls who cannot wait to heal enough to climb back on, and I have known a few riders who scarcely got more than a bruise who never rode again. Fear is where you find it. So is the absence of fear (fig. 4.3). But most riders who have had broken bones and a prolonged recovery period will understandably have a certain degree of caution and apprehension as the day gets closer to actually getting back on another horse, or often worse, the horse they came off when they got hurt.

4.3: While in her seventies, Mrs. Fletcher Harper rode in several GMHA 100-Mile rides with the "wrong" leg across her side saddle because of an old hip fracture. She recovered both strength and courage to carry on.

Strategies for Regaining Confidence

So what are some strategies that can help ease the transition from being a wounded victim to being once again a confident rider?

Well, the very first thing to consider is how fully you have healed and recovered. If your doctor has recommended that you give your broken ankle three months to fully heal and repair, and you are riding again after nine weeks, you know darn well that you are playing Russian roulette because of your lack of patience. An injury that isn't fully healed is vulnerable to re-injury, and unless you are sort of a reckless type of brave, this knowledge will likely cause you some trepidation. Better to give the injury time to heal, and then give your body time to get back in shape from the condition it lost while the injury prevented you from engaging in your regular level of activity.

> If you are unwilling to accept that you can change and learn and grow, if you are too arrogant, too sure that what you think is right, just because you think it, you will probably stay inept and incompetent.
>
> ■ ■ ■

I have had two broken hips and a broken neck, and those necessitated long layoffs from normal athletic workouts. I started to recover by doing lots of work around the farm without riding, like cutting riding trails, hauling brush, things that made me work and pant and use muscles that had become slack from inactivity. By the time I was ready to ride again, the breaks had healed, and I was pretty physically fit and in shape.

The next part of the recovery strategy is to absolutely not get back on a horse that is tough to ride, and the worse you have been hurt, and the more you have been scared, the more you should start on a docile and nonreactive horse. In really bad cases, set up some sessions at a therapeutic riding center, with horses that are steady enough to deal with badly impaired riders. You may only need to get in a few rides with these bombproof horses before you feel your confidence returning, but if that's what you need, do the smart thing.

Absolutely understand that your recovery is yours, not someone else's. You should not be shamed or pressured into doing things that make you uncomfortable, nor should you think in terms of any timetable. You will be ready to do more when you are ready. And if you are not ready, don't do something you don't want to just because it's something you "ought" to. The hell with "ought." It's your choice what you decide to do, and if you decide to take time off from riding, or give up riding altogether, that is your choice, and nobody else needs to have a say in the matter.

Usually, though, if you are smart about getting back into riding gradually, you will feel your confidence returning. Don't be pressured into riding the tougher horses, though, or galloping fast, or jumping, or doing harder things until you begin to feel so bored at the level you are doing that it becomes your choice and your decision to do more.

I guess the best way I know to boil this down into a simple answer is to reiterate this: It is no one else's recovery, just yours. Take all the time you need. If you get back to your prior level, great. If you don't, you don't. But you need to be the one making the decision.

Don't Believe Your Own Press

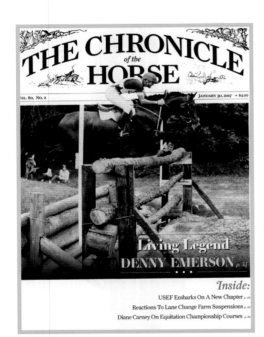

4.4: **Bill Steinkraus told me that when you do well, people praise you too highly, and when you do poorly, people criticize you too harshly, so you should basically ignore what people say or write about you.**

When you are young and green, you may be brave and cocky, and you may win lots of blue ribbons, and you may even get your picture on some horse magazine covers, but the chances are high that you will also be inept and incompetent about many things pertaining to horses, no matter how many people fawn over you and tell you how good you are (fig. 4.4).

I look back at photos from the 1960s and '70s, never mind from the '50s, when I thought I had a clue, and I know beyond a shadow of a doubt that much of what I thought then was not only wrong, it was based on bad horsemanship.

And if you are unwilling to accept that you can change and learn and grow, if you are too arrogant, too sure that what you think is right, just because you think it, you will probably stay inept and incompetent.

I suspect that deep down, many riders suspect

that they are "frauds" in some fundamental ways, and some will have the guts to face up to that, and will struggle to become better, and some will keep up the façade.

There is an old saying, "Don't believe your own press."

The Barn Rat Route

Unlike their furry gray namesakes, these barn rats come in various shapes, ages, and sizes, the most common being girls between the ages of about 10 or 11 to somewhere in the mid to late teens. They are reasonably easy to identify in their native habitat, which is any variant of horse barn (fig. 4.5). Barn rats are the horse-crazy kids who don't want to be anywhere else. Not at the mall, not at the fast food joint, not even (sometimes) at the junior prom if there's a horse show the next day.

Some barn rats get paid, but many trade work for the chance just to be in the general vicinity of horses. The parents of barn rats can't be the obsessive kind who drag their kids from piano lessons to French lessons to figure

4.5: "Barn rats" are the kids who hang out at barns. They learn by osmosis. There is no better way, none, nyet, nein, not any....

skating lessons to soccer practice, because implicit in the definition of "barn rats" is that they spend most free moments—after school, on weekends, and on vacations—at the barn.

Barn rats are not the kids who arrive at the stable, take their lessons or ride their horses, get back in the car and disappear. A kid doesn't have to be "from the poor side of town" to be a card-carrying barn rat, because it's a state of mind more than socioeconomic status that differentiates the real deal from the pretender. True barn rats would hang around the barn and do manual labor even if they won the lottery, because that's what taking care of horses really means.

Weather Wimps and Other Whiney Creatures

So it's Saturday, April 28, 2012, 4:30 a.m. By 7:30, we need to be on the GMHA grounds to be vetted in for the Mud Ride, and it's 27 miles of bad road between South Woodstock and Strafford, Vermont, and the three mares we are taking are outside and need to be caught, brought in, fed, loaded, and hauled to the ride. I note that it's pitch black outside, I hear the wind moaning off the hill, and I check the thermometer: 24 degrees Fahrenheit, a heat wave compared to the predicted 22. Outside, in the yard, I notice flakes of fine snow caught in the windshield wipers, and in the overhead lights, I can see random flakes blowing horizontally against the black bulk of the barn. I think to myself, "This could be a long day."

Flick back 20 years to late April, 1992, at what was then the Rolex Kentucky Three-Day Event. The Kentucky Horse Park in Lexington: I woke up at 5:00 a.m. and heard heavy rain pelting against my window. Munching hay, warm and dry in stalls, Epic Win and Griffin were unaware that in a few hours they would be galloping around in that slop with, unfortunately, me on top telling them, more or less, where they were supposed to go (fig. 4.6).

Later, as I walked around the collecting ring on my first ride, Griffin, with

4.6: It is okay to whine and snivel about the weather, as long as you get out and ride in that weather that you whine and snivel about. Many years ago I was told, "Denny, it always rains in England. If the English riders only rode in good weather, they would not be the number-one riding country in the world."

cold rain finding its way through the minute flaws in my rain gear and trickling down my back, I looked up to see fellow competitor Ralph Hill, looking like some deranged pirate, walking beside me. Rain was dripping off both points of his moustache, off his ponytail, and glistened off his gold earring. He gave me a manic grin and announced, "Another day at the office!"

And I thought, "This could be a long day."

A GMHA Mud Ride was the start of my fifty-ninth consecutive season of competing in horse events, so I've had lots of those "this could be a long day" mornings, and I have never learned to like them, and I've never missed a chance to whine and complain about the weather. Especially when it's early-morning bad weather. Before-coffee bad weather. Wet, cold, bad weather. Cold, windy, bad weather. Cold, wet, windy, early-morning, dark, before-coffee-with-little-hope-of-redemption bad weather.

Personally, I think it's a mark of flawed character to be stoic and brave about adverse weather conditions.

■ ■ ■

Personally, I think it's a mark of flawed character to be stoic and brave about adverse weather conditions. Can't those people see that mud, all that snow, that rain, the trees bending in the wind? Are they oblivious to the cold, the feeling of soaked breeches, the water in their boots?

"Wimps of the world, unite!" is my motto. Why fight it? If it's too hot, too wet, too dusty, too cold, too muddy, too rainy, too snowy, too windy, at least have the good grace to whine about it. Let others be brave and feel all superior. I prefer to snivel!

It Only Matters if It Matters to You

Like many of us, I get to see lots of horse magazines and books, and usually their primary emphasis is on the higher levels of whatever horse sport they promote. I see photos of the same relatively few riders over and over and get to read about the bigger competitions.

This emphasis on the upper levels can easily lead to the perception that competitions at lower levels are somehow inherently less "worthy" than those that are more difficult. If going Beginner Novice in eventing is entry level then, according to this line of reasoning, it's better to go Novice, better still to ride at the Training Level, and transcendently better to ride at the Kentucky Three-Day Event.

It's harder, that's for sure, to ride at the upper levels, but "better" is a most subjective word. I was aware of this subjectivity when I wrote *How Good Riders Get Good*, because a good rider is simply a good rider, no

4.7: You start out riding as a kid. Where you go, or don't go from that point on is your business. Not your friends' business. Not your parents' business. Your business.

more, no less. The intrinsic worth of that person is tied up in her ability to ride well only if she is judged according to that narrow standard. If it matters strongly to someone to be a good rider, then it matters. If it doesn't matter, then it doesn't matter (fig. 4.7).

Years ago, I read an article about a couple of riding instructors who were talking negatively about a not very fit, not very expert rider whom they both found difficult to teach. They made the usual comments. You can well imagine those, I'm sure. A couple of days later, the young son of one of the trainers was riding his bike and was struck by a car, and it was that not-so-great rider, in her other role—as a doctor—who saved that child's life.

Does it matter how good a rider someone is, in the greater scheme? Only if it matters to that individual. Apart from that, enjoy the level where you find fulfillment. And if you want to get to a higher level, by all means, struggle along, but don't feel that anyone cares very strongly, one way or the other, except, as that old saying goes, "you and your mother."

Young Riders, Old Riders

"The old horses make the young riders. The old riders make the young horses."

(The words "old" and "young" here are in terms of experience more than chronological age.)

This is one of the most profound yet most ignored old sayings in the world of riding. What does it actually mean?

Teach Him vs. Make Him

We all know that a horse can feel it when a fly lands on him because he instantly swishes his tail at the annoyance. And as I discussed in chapter three, we can use this knowledge to create various conditioned responses by using very light aids to teach the horse that when he moves away from a light pressure, that light pressure will go away.

I've mentioned that what I used to do, for far too many years (partly because I did not know any better, and because I had actually been taught to do it) was to escalate the intensity of my pressure, instead of sort of quietly "pestering" the horse with light pressures until he began to learn that the way to get rid of the mildly annoying pressure was to move away from it (see p. 78 for my explanation of "pestering.") What I failed to realize back then was that by ramping up the intensity of my leg pressure, for example, while I did get the result of him moving away from it, I had obtained the result I wanted with a substantially negative byproduct. Yes, he moved off my kicking leg, but the sharpness of my kicks had made him more nervous and anxious. Now I had to deal with a more reactive horse, which meant that very often I would feel the need for stronger rein contact to control the nervousness

Say a young rider is riding a trained horse (he's that "programmed computer" we created in chapter three), and in the attempt to learn how to ride better somewhat randomly and inexpertly applies a variety of aids to elicit a right lead canter. (Read: "Hits random buttons.") Sort of by mistake, the rider hits the right lead canter button, and the horse picks up a right lead canter. Before too long, that young rider has figured out that the way to get the right lead canter is to apply certain pressures. The well-trained horse responds, providing positive feedback to the learning rider.

Now take an "old" rider on a "young" horse. The rider knows what buttons to push (aids to apply) to get a right lead canter, so the rider applies

that I had actually created. As I used stronger rein contact, the horse got even more nervous, and the downward training spiral had begun.

What I was doing was *forcing* the move-away response rather than *teaching* the move-away response. If I had sort of mildly poked and pestered him, and not been in such a hurry to get an instant response, the horse would have "put two and two together" and realized that the way to get rid of the mildly annoying pressure was to move away from it, but in a way that was far less nervous and reactive than how he had been when I booted him hard to make him do it.

Sure, most riding books do not call aids "mildly annoying pressures,"

In this photo, Carrie Ramsey is asking her young OTTB mare Saroca to move away from mild pressure.

but then, if not, what are they? Heck, anything we do other than let our horse stand and eat "annoys" him! But low-intensity pressures can teach. High-intensity pressures are more likely to coerce. Think for yourself which type of trainer you want to be.

those aids. If the horse responds by cantering off on the right lead, the rider "thanks" the horse by softening the stimulus. If the horse runs into a left lead canter, the rider brings the horse back to a trot, and reapplies the same set of aids, correcting when the horse responds wrong, softening when the horse gets it correctly.

The old horse "programs" the young rider to apply the correct aids—in all sorts of situations, to produce the desired response. The old rider "programs" the young horse by applying the correct aids—in all sorts of situations, to provide the correct response.

It is so simple. Why is this so often ignored? Partly ignorance; partly arrogance. Those are two of the reasons.

A Horse's Future Depends on the Human Who Owns Him

Over many years, the main thing I have started to figure out about the highly complex interaction between humans and domesticated horses is that humans call the shots, and the horses basically must do what the humans choose, be that right or wrong for the well-being of the horses.

Each human will have his or her own moral compass as to what they will or will not ask the horse to do.

■ ■ ■

And that each human will have his or her own moral compass as to what they will or will not ask the horse to do.

And that a human can have a "good" moral compass, but if the human is not horse savvy, good intentions can lead to unintended bad results.

And that most humans make some sort of tradeoff with the horse, as in, "I will feed you, and provide you with a good life, but in exchange, you will let me ride or drive you for a certain amount of time each week."

And some humans, guided by a kind moral compass and a true understanding of biomechanics and overall horse care, will carefully prepare the

4.8: For a short while only, the little foal finds safety and security at the side of his dam. The future life of the young horse will in large part be determined by the human who acquires him. Whether he will have a good life or a life of stress and pain will be up to the knowledge, empathy, and compassion of that human.

horse to withstand the stresses that the riding or driving will put on the horse, so that the tradeoff is fair (fig. 4.8).

Some riders will be so competitively driven, though, or money hungry or glory hungry or simply ignorant, that they will push the horse harder and harder, in ways that lead the horse to live a life of fear and stress and even pain, injury, and suffering.

And these are not choices made by the horses, but by the humans who control their fate. So each human has to decide what choices he or she will make for the horses under his or her control.

The Best Trainers

Someone asked me if I would take a shot at listing the traits the greatest trainers have in common, and as they say, fools rush in where angels fear to tread, so the following are some that I feel many of the great ones have. There are no doubt others, and different trainers will have varying priorities.

The very best trainers don't say "bad horse."

They will look for real reasons when a horse seems to be struggling to get it. It might be pain or discomfort related, poor saddle fit, poor choice of bit, lack of understanding of what is being asked, prior rough treatment, lack of adequate fitness—there are so many possibilities (fig. 4.9).

The best trainers know better than to expect much from any given training session on any given day.

The best trainers seem not to work against the clock. They have no time-based agenda. It will take as long as it takes.

The best trainers always try to avoid using force or coercion.

The best trainers use a slow warm-up, with gentle stretches, creating a flexible, almost "slinky" movement from the horse.

The best trainers have learned to think "good" for sort of good, sometimes even for sort of okay. They get a sliver of improvement and then quit while they are ahead.

4.9: The very greatest horse trainers, like former Swedish Olympic dressage coach Walter Christensen here (standing behind the horse), never say, "That horse is being bad." Never. Not ever....

The best trainers never end a training session with a "fried" horse.

Generally, the best trainers are always open to finding better ways to do it better. They are open, rather than know-it-alls, and training for them is always something in flux, in transition, a process rather than a formula.

Bonfire and the GMHA 100-Mile Competitive Trail Ride

By the fall of 1954 I'd turned 13, and it was becoming clear that while I had grown several inches over the past three years, Paint had not. I was getting to the inevitable point when I was outgrowing my first pony. Luckily, Paint was such a great pony that there were lots of little kids who wanted him, so it was easy to find him a wonderful home.

And so, back to Louis Goodyear's in October we went, on the hunt for the next horse. I think that Paint was probably 14 or 14.1 hands, and the new horse I found, probably mostly Quarter Horse, was closer to 15.1 or 15.2. I'd just finished reading Walter Farley's *The Black Stallion's Sulky Colt* about a blood bay named Bonfire, so I stole that name for my new horse (fig. 4.10).

There was a magazine rack in the Stoneleigh-Prospect Hill School library, where I found a copy of the Green Mountain Horse Association magazine, full of articles about something called a "100-mile trail ride." In the ride, there was a "junior division," and although my sum total of knowledge about conditioning for distance rides amounted to zero, I decided that I would enter the ride. I duly requested an entry form for the 1955 ride, which was almost a year in the future, and got a reply from the GMHA office that my name was on the list to receive an entry when they came out the following spring.

Peter Haubrich, a boy about my age, had written an article in that same GMHA magazine based on the idea that for each mile of a competitive ride, it was important to have done about 10 miles of prior conditioning. If you want to do a 100-mile ride, you should condition for 1,000 miles beforehand.

4.10: When I switched from first pony to first horse, I didn't switch very dramatically. Bonfire was only about 15.1 or so, and like my first pony Paint, he was calm and forgiving. Here we are at the preliminary judging on the day before the GMHA 100-Mile ride in 1956.

Since I had only gotten Bonfire a month or so before, I figured I'd better put off my 100-mile goal from 1955 to 1956, and get busy adding up those 1,000 miles. Here are some actual, verbatim entries from two diaries I kept, one from 1955, and one from 1956. Bear with me here. There may even be a reason for you to read all this (as you'll see at the end)!

Saturday, January 1, 1955 (I was 14.)
The blacksmith came and winter shod all the school horses and Bon-fire. We skated in the afternoon and played hockey. The ice was very smooth. Tommy (my brother) fell in, but the water was not deep.

Sunday, January 2, 1955

It was very rainy and it snowed a little during the night. Brenda's horse came. It is a Palomino mare. I went riding in the afternoon. It was very slippery in some places.

Monday, January 3, 1955

Francis brought Scottie's horse back. Jack came up and we went riding. Jack rode Paul's horse. I rode Bonfire. There was some skating, but it was not too safe around the edges.

Tuesday, January 4, 1955

It snowed during the night. The Steele's horses came back. So did Barhyte's horse. It is a new one called Don. I went riding in the morning. The blacksmith came and shod Vaun. All the girls came back from vacation. Later at night Pepper Q and Shanney came back.

Thursday, January 6, 1955

I went to school. We got out early because of rain. I brushed my horse. Riding was impossible because everything was glare ice.

Saturday, January 8, 1955

Doug, Joe, Paul, and Danny came down. We played hockey all morning. In the afternoon went riding. I used a new bridle on Bonfire.

Sunday, January 9, 1955

Ken Seul and John Donovan came over from the meadows. We went riding. Tommy and a lot of other kids skated. The bridle doesn't work too well.

Saturday, January 15, 1955

It snowed. We only got about 2 inches. I rode up to Bernardston. It was very cold—8 degrees. The girls are painting the tack room. The colors are brown (the walls) and red.

Sunday, January 16, 1955

I went to church. Judy Harwood's horse was supposed to come, but it failed to arrive. In the afternoon some of the girls and I rode over to Bob's. He sold his horse because it had the heaves.

Lots of blank pages follow, as I must have lost the energy to keep up with my diary. Then, six months later, this one:

Wednesday, July 11, 1955

I rode Bonfire up beyond Bernardston. It took four hours. Then I harrowed. Then I helped Francis put up the new pasture fence.

Up until the summer of 1955, I had only ridden Western or bareback, but some of the little horse shows had English classes, and, in my greed for ribbons, I started using an English saddle on Bonfire some of the time so that I could compete in more classes.

> At 14, I was already obsessed with horses, and I seemed to have been goal-oriented, neither of which states have changed much over the succeeding decades.
>
> ■ ■ ■

Reading these old diary entries from six decades earlier reminds me of the saying that, "The child is the father to the man." At 14, I was already obsessed with horses, and I seemed to have been goal-oriented, neither of which states have changed much over the succeeding decades.

In 1956, I made a few more attempts at keeping a diary. Both the 1955 and 1956 versions are little maroon books sent presumably to my parents by John C. Paige and Company Insurance, 40 Broad Street, Boston. By that time I was away at boarding school, a junior (Andover's term for freshman) at Phillips Academy in Andover, Massachusetts. I was at home for Christmas vacation when the New Year rolled in.

Sunday, January 1, 1956

Dad and I split some logs up at school and loaded them on the pile near the fireplace. I went riding in the afternoon. Bonfire was feeling good and we had quite a time.

Monday, January 2, 1956

I went riding in the morning. In the afternoon we measured the route to Bernardston. It is 11 miles round trip. Helen Woodhull's horse arrived. Jack's father bought a horse.

Later, spring vacation entries:

Wednesday, March 21, 1956

I went riding in the morning. The snow was so deep in places that Bonfire had trouble getting through. Later, I put him out in the paddock, and he rolled about 10 times.

By then it was June of 1956. I was out of school for the summer and could set my sights directly on the GMHA 100-mile trail ride coming up in three months. I can't remember, all these years later, what kind of physical shape Bonfire was in when I got home from Andover, but I can only assume that he'd been in work with one or more of the Stoneleigh girls that winter and spring. At any rate, a few more diary entries:

Thursday, June 7, 1956

First day of vacation. I slept fairly late this morning, and ate breakfast at about eleven o'clock, after I had been riding about an hour or so. I went up through Coomb's pasture and then down past Brownie's Trailer Camp. Bonfire seems to be in good condition for the amount of work he has done, but there is a long way to go.

"A long way to go." That's a relatively mature reflection, I think, for a 14-year-old kid. At any rate, a few more sporadic diary entries, including a 17-mile ride from Greenfield to Whately on June 11 to visit Jack Baker. I can vaguely remember lots of rides up Swamp Road to Bernardston, but 60 years ago was a long time, so details are vague. At any rate, on Tuesday, August 28, 1956, eight days after my fifteenth birthday, we loaded Bonfire into our homemade, open-topped, two-wheeled, wooden, one-horse trailer, and arrived at the Woodstock Inn Stables from Greenfield that afternoon. My diary entries were brief:

Wednesday, August 29, 1956
Horse judged in.

Thursday, August 30, 1956
First day of ride.

Friday, August 31, 1956
Rained all day.

Saturday, September 1, 1956
Finished ride at GMHA.

Lessons Learned

And that was it for 1956 diary entries. So what did I learn? More to the point, what do I look back on and realize that I learned, so that I might be in a position to give some thoughts, ideas, and advice in a book written 60 years after the fact?

Well, one big thing that I realize about my individual learning style, not just from this diary but from numerous subsequent quests and decisions made over following years, is that I just plunge in and learn as I go. And so can you. And so can anyone who wants something badly enough.

When I was 13, and first read about the GMHA 100-Mile, and decided on the spot that I would ride in it, it was a decision based upon nothing more than early teenage ignorance and, probably the right word, a degree of teenage arrogance. I decided to do it because I wanted to do it. And there are worse ways, I think. If I had done this the rational, measured, objective way, I would have spent several years learning all about distance riding, conditioning programs, trail riding, and maybe I would and maybe I would not have ever done the GMHA ride.

And if I hadn't done the GMHA ride in 1956, my parents would not have gotten interested in buying property in the area. They wouldn't have bought their farm in South Reading in 1957, and I wouldn't have met the people who introduced me to eventing four years later, and I wouldn't be writing this book.

So sometimes the impetuous way works. It often has for me. Decide what it is that you want to do, and immediately take the first steps that are likely to take you where you want to go. Absolutely, you will make mistakes. Inevitably you will encounter plenty of error in this kind of trial and error path. But you will have started. Lots of people never get anywhere because they never start.

So, start, don't be afraid of messing up, and see where it takes you. Don't dither, dabble around, fuss, question, and procrastinate. Learn this W.H. Murray quote (Murray, a mountaineer and author, nailed the idea of commitment as well as anyone I know):

Until one is committed there is hesitancy, the chance to draw back, always ineffectiveness. Concerning all acts of initiative (and creation) there is one elementary truth, the ignorance of which kills countless ideas and splendid plans: that the moment one definitely commits oneself, then Providence moves too. All sorts of things occur to help one that would never otherwise have occurred.

Chestry Oak

When I was a freshman at Dartmouth College, in the fall of 1959, I met a timber-horse breeder from Woodstock, Vermont, named Mac Williamson. Normally, Vermont would be about the last place to meet someone so keen on racing over fences, but Mac had a couple of flat horses at Rockingham and some jumpers down in Southern Pines, North Carolina.

During my four years at college, as I got more involved with Thoroughbreds and with jumping, I used to drive over to Mac's High Pastures Farm to ride horses by stallions such as Cormac, who had been a Maryland Hunt Cup near winner until he severed

When you have a mare (Chee Oaks) and a stallion (Core Buff) and breed them to produce a foal (Chestry Oak), and later ride that foal around big Advanced tracks like Ledyard and Chesterland and Kentucky, you have done something that not many riders or trainers have managed to accomplish. Apart from riding in events at the Preliminary level, or higher, for 50 consecutive seasons, this was probably the hardest goal I ever set and realized.

a tendon on a beer bottle near the race finish.

Mac had a broodmare named Chee Oaks, by the top timber and chasing sire, Hunters Moon 4th. Chee Oaks, who had herself been a stakes winner over brush, was a strongly made, plain bay mare. Years later, after Mac died, Mrs. Williamson gave Chee Oaks to my wife May and me, to be our first Thoroughbred broodmare. We had a young stallion named Core Buff, also from Maryland Hunt Cup lines, as his dam, Royal Cor, was by Cormac. We bred Chee Oaks to Core Buff, and in the spring of 1974, Chee produced a bay filly we named Chestry Oak.

I think it's pretty normal, when a foal is born, to invest that baby with all sorts of hopes and dreams, but as stark reality suggests, most of those dreams never come true. That reality didn't stop me from hoping that baby Chestry would some day live up to what I thought of as her breeding destiny.

As she grew from newborn to yearling to first-ridden three-year-old to Novice eventer to Training eventer to Preliminary winner, Chestry Oak kept stepping up and stepping up, and she just kept doing so, all the way to jumping a clear round at the 1985 Rolex Kentucky Three-Day Event.

I had ridden her sire, Core Buff, at the Kentucky Three-Day a few years earlier, and I don't know of another father-daughter pair that has ever done this. They tell you that to take a homebred to the upper levels is a most fulfilling accomplishment, and guess what? They're right.

In Retrospect: What I'd Do Differently with Chestry Oak

What's the saying? "Tell a gelding, ask a mare, negotiate with a stallion?"

Chestry Oak was a mare that needed a lot more asking from me and a lot less telling.

I was, in the 1970s, still too much a proponent of the platitudes I had learned 20 years earlier. Sayings like, "Show him who's boss," and "Don't let him get away with that" (totally inappropriate for any horse, never mind a sensitive Thoroughbred mare) were my go-to concepts of training strategies. Just as with Cat, Victor, York, and all my earlier horses, I should have been vastly more patient, much softer, more conciliatory, but I simply did not know.

I look back on horses like Chestry Oak and think, if only I had that do-over button—how differently I would approach them all.

A whole stream of events issues from the decision, raising in one's favor all manner of unforeseen, incidents and meetings and material assistance, which no man would have dreamed would come his way.

I have learned a deep respect for one of Goethe's couplets, "Whatever you can do, or dream you can, begin it. Boldness has genius, power and magic in it."

Back when I was 14 and 15, I wouldn't be reading the Murray quote for another half a century. Somehow, though, I must have sensed at some subliminal level one of the great truths. You can't finish what you don't begin.

> Lots of people never get anywhere because they never start.
> ■ ■ ■

Forever and ever I listen to people talking and lamenting about how they "want to do this," "hope to do that," "wish to do the other," never managing to commit themselves to taking that critical first step. I didn't know much at age 13, when I wrote to the GMHA for an entry form. But that simple act of getting a piece of paper, getting an envelope, getting a two-cent stamp, changed everything. The total commitment came later, but the first step had been taken.

If I could advise only one thing in this entire book, it would be something I figured out for myself. "Take the first step."

5

A Rider's Physical Skills

The Riding Body

All humans come with certain physical characteristics that are beyond their control. These include someone's age, height, and general bone structure—what we call someone's "build." But beyond factors like these, most of us have some degree of control over what we are, physically, and what we can train our body to be able to do.

Most athletes know about general fitness. They often have exercise programs like running, weightlifting, pushups, squats, pull-ups, and sit-ups to increase strength, stamina, endurance, and agility. These are basic to most sports, not just to riding sports.

A rider needs balance to deal with the constantly shifting motion of the moving horse. She needs flexible strength, rather than rigid strength. Most good riders are strong enough to deal with the demands of a sometimes unpredictable 1,000-pound animal, but that strength tends to be lithe strength, fluid and supple, almost snake-like in its "slithery" ability to adapt instantly to the body beneath her, somewhat like the strength needed by the surfer or the downhill ski racer.

In addition to the basic elements we find in common with athletes in a multitude of sports, there are very specific physical skill sets that are required by the various kinds of horse sports, and these may vary enormously, sport by sport. I have a son who is a calf roper. He has to race after the calf, throw a rope, catch the calf, stop his horse, leap off the right side of the horse, run down the rope, catch, flank, and throw the struggling calf, gather three legs, and tie them in a way that the calf can't break loose. Every single part of that sequence involves all kinds of distinct physical skills, and someone riding in a dressage test does not have to possess any of them.

> Do not get conned into one person's definition of the phrase "good rider," as if only one way constitutes the one true path to riding nirvana.
>
> ■ ■ ■

The dressage rider has to have her own quiver full of specific skill sets, different but equally difficult. She needs to know how to put a horse on the aids, how to perform movements like leg-yield, half-pass, shoulder-in, haunches-in, haunches-out, flying changes, and, at the higher levels, passage and piaffe.

The jumping rider needs still other skill sets, as does the reiner, the endurance racer, the cutting horse rider, and the polo player.

It is not my intention in the section that follows to go in great depth about many specific physical skills, other than to point out something quite basic. If you were an archer, back in the days of Robin Hood, and you were firing arrows at attacking warriors and you reached back over your shoulder to pluck out another arrow, and your quiver was empty, you had darn well better be a fast runner.

The more you can fill your skill quiver with skill sets, the better trainer and rider you will be (fig. 5.1). Sure, you won't always be at the height of your overall physical powers. I read recently in someone's blog about peak powers, "You're only 25 once. Then you are, and then you aren't." So you can't worry

5.1: As a role model for lifelong physical fitness, Walt Gervais is hard to beat. A boxing champion in the US Navy in 1942, twenty-fifth in the Boston Marathon in 1946, it would be 50 years later, at the age of 75, that Walt would compete in his first Preliminary level, long-format Three-Day event, at Bromont in Canada. Here he is with me in the starting gate for the steeplechase on Timmy.

about the things over which you have no control. But you have enormous control over most everything else if you decide to learn what you need and then practice to hone these skills so that they are in your quiver when you reach back over your shoulder, so to speak, to draw them out.

What Does It Mean, "So-and-So Is a Good Rider?"

It depends on the specific interest of the person who says it.

A bronc rider says it about another bronc rider, a dressage rider about another dressage rider, an endurance rider about another endurance rider, and so on, and each of them will be right, but only in a limited way, because "good rider" can mean good about a realm of different skills and abilities. So do not get conned into one person's definition of the phrase "good rider," as if only one way constitutes the one true path to riding nirvana.

The show jumper who defines "good" believes one thing, and the working-cow competitor believes something entirely different, and I will bet $32 million that the riders who are considered champions in each of these two riding sports would not even have a clue about the names of the champions in the other.

So, brag and boast all you want about your rider in your sport, but realize that in another sport, your rider's name will elicit a "Who?" and nothing more.

Elasticity, and How "Trying" Kills It

Most great athletes are elastic. They are flexible and supple and, as I said earlier, sometimes almost snake-like in the way their body can move and slink and flow. I've heard it said that if you want your horse to move like a panther, you have to move like a panther, with all your joints and muscles fluid and flexible rather than tight and stiff (fig. 5.2). We've talked about how the best riders almost seem to be moving, breathing extensions of the horses they ride, as if the spinal column of the horse and the spinal column of the human had merged.

We can get more by pretending we want less.

■ ■ ■

But here's a problem, or at least the threat of a problem, because we have been taught that the avenue to improvement is to try harder. I think it's difficult to try hard to ride better while at the same time staying flexible and elastic, because the effort of trying hard creates a degree of tension and anxiety: "I have to do this well. I need to get this right."

Tension and anxiety kill elasticity, the one thing we actually need the most. So what to do? I asked a friend about this one time, and his answer was, "Drink heavily, ha-ha-ha."

While that might alleviate some degree of tension, I don't think getting

5.2: Reputed Testamony, in panther mode. Rep raced 55 times, and won the Maryland Million Classic.

hammered before climbing on a horse is the ideal way to go to avoid being tight and nervous.

One key strategy is to ride a horse that is tolerant of our mistakes while we get to the point where we can be more elastic and harmonious. If every time we inadvertently lurch or wobble and we set off the horse, all it will do is make us tighter and less elastic.

Another thing is to play the "I don't care" mind game. We do care. We do want to improve. Why else would we take lessons or practice? But we need to act as if we don't have such a stake in the process. Get more by pretending we want less. Not all riders can manage to "play" this game, but it's a useful exercise if you can do it.

Another way is to spend so much time riding that you can't sustain being nervous. I don't care if you are a total "Nervous Nellie" with a death grip of cast iron on the reins and a face rigid with anxiety—if you ride five or six hours a day for five or six days, by the end of each day you will be so tired, and probably so sore, that worrying about the horse will be the least of your concerns. Most riders have never been exposed to this "total immersion" theory of anxiety alleviation, but—no joke—it works. Go on a pack trip out West, or on a multi-day endurance ride, 40 or 50 miles a day for several days, and see how it starts to feel normal. It is an honest-to-God real strategy if all else seems to be failing.

All of these methods to become a "silkier," more elastic rider involve actually plunking your seat in a saddle and riding a horse. We are not going to "hope" our way to elasticity. Repeat after me: It is just not going to happen. We need to get on and ride.

Slither Woman

Words that convey the ways in which all the good riders melt into the movement of their horse are slithery, slinky, snake-like, so that if someone says about you, "Hey, girl, you look like Slither Woman on that horse," that is about the best compliment you are going to get all year.

I was watching a former NFR (National Finals Rodeo) bareback champion out in Sheridan, Wyoming, riding a colt across a big pasture, and he and that horse were in such total harmony they resembled one being, like a centaur. I said as much to the old rancher who owned the colt, and the guy replied, "That boy has always had ball bearings in his hips."

When I would watch Bruce Davidson riding any of his immense string of horses, I was always struck by how all his body parts—arms, hips, knees, ankles—seemed to "flow" with the movements of the horses. Another top rider made the comment, "I wish my arms were as soft as Bruce's. They look like a pair of writhing snakes on a hot rock."

And, while the idea of being a snake on a horse may strike some as maybe not the most complimentary comment, it is actually high praise

Bareback Riding

Kendall Szumilas riding the former racehorse Meet In Khartoum, a mare by Pioneer of the Nile, also sire of recent Triple Crown winner American Pharoah.

've never read anything about riding without a saddle in any book about dressage, show jumping, or eventing. But kids who spend hours playing around bareback on ponies will have gained all sorts of advantages that their more "formally" raised counterparts never get.

Far back in the history of riding, before saddles were even invented, mounted warriors, hunters, and herdsmen in the various horse cultures rode bareback, and today we think of those riders as being intuitively and mindlessly merged into the bodies of their horses, almost "slithering" in their abilities.

When you are a small child, walking, trotting, and cantering over all sorts of terrain without a saddle, you aren't likely to get "paralyzed" by trying too hard to "do it correctly." You are learning to ride in the most natural way of all, by just riding. The more you ride, the more your body and your horse's body blend as one creature.

Later, if more formal riding becomes a goal, the hard part of learning is already over, and you will scarcely have noticed while you were doing it that you were actually even learning.

when you consider the various alternatives, like stiff, awkward, rigid, fixed, and so forth.

Go watch the riders that you most aspire to be like, and I will be surprised if you cannot discern a "slippery" quality in the way their body meshes with the body of the horse they sit on, to the point that they do not sit "on" the horse as much as they and the horse appear to become one entity.

An Independent Seat

As your body gradually attunes itself to the movements of that larger body beneath you, you will be in the process of developing what is known as "an independent seat." So let's talk about what is meant by that word "independent." A seat independent of what?

"Seats"

There are all sorts of "seats": hunt seat, balanced seat, saddle seat, dressage seat, cross-country seat, Western seat, and on and on. Each type of seat has a purpose and a goal, so the first thing to decide is what kind of riding you need a certain seat "for."

The two most opposite seats, dressage and steeplechase jockey, can best be described as angles and the absence of angles.

The dressage rider sits erect, with long stirrups, so that if you took the horse away from the picture, the dressage rider would almost look to be standing up, with few closed angles. Conversely, if you removed the horse out from under the 'chase jockey, he would be seen as "squatting," with tightly closed ankle, knee and hip angles.

Both take athleticism with core strength for the dressage rider to absorb the concussive effects of the horse's swinging back, and flexible strength for the jockey to hold and balance 1,100-hundred-dred pounds of hurtling horse.

For best results, create the agile and supple seat for your sport. Flopping and lurching like a sodden rag doll is probably the sort of connection with your horse's back you'd prefer to avoid.

Stirrups, that's what.

When you have stirrups, you can post at the trot and hover at the canter and ride your entire life never having to train your body to absorb the concussive motion of the horse's back. Granted, the poster who can't sit the trot will not be as skilled a rider as the poster who *can* sit the trot, but if you don't care, we don't care. However, if you want to do some sport that requires sitting the trot, like dressage or eventing, you'll be up the creek until you learn how to do it.

You don't post at the canter, of course, but you can avoid the thumps and bumps induced in the horse's back when he canters by getting into what is known as a "half-seat" or "two-point position." Here, you slightly stand in your stirrups and "hover" over the motion so that you can avoid it.

Dressage seat: Carrie Ramsey on Beaulieu's Cool Concorde (A). Galloping seat: Kendall Szumilas on Beaulieu's Cool Attitude (B).

So, "independent" of the need for stirrups is one answer.

Another way to define "independent seat" is to think of the middle part of your body as the seat part. This is your pelvis, which includes your actual seat bones, your stomach and lower back up to where your short ribs start, and your thighs down to your knees. This "seat part" is made possible by the fact that your pelvis can rotate forward and back because it isn't hitched by rigid bone to your upper torso or to your legs.

Your stomach is attached by muscles. Your lower back, same thing. Each thigh has a ball and socket joint so there is tremendous flexibility and range of motion.

Sally Swift, the author of *Centered Riding,* used to say that your middle from just below your short ribs down to your knees—your "stubby legs"— belongs to the horse, so that the rest of your body can belong to you (fig. 5.3). In other words, the main part of a rider that constitutes that "independent seat" is that whole middle part. This lets you move your lower legs independently. Your hands and arms and torso and neck and head are independent, too. Your middle takes and absorbs the hits, so that the rest of your body can move "independently."

So, the seat is "independent" of needing the use of the stirrups, and the seat is "independent" of your other body parts.

CENTERED
RIDING
by Sally Swift

OVER
150,000
IN PRINT

"*Wonderfully imaginative in finding just the right psychological images
to go beyond the mere mechanics of riding...indispensable.*"
—William Steinkraus

5.3: Sally Swift's astute insights into the way the human body moves, and her gentle teaching style, and her towering best seller, *Centered Riding,* have helped thousands of riders unlock the elasticity within their own bodies.

A Modest Idea About Human Fitness

At an event recently, it was easy to see about 8 to 10 cross-country jumps from the knoll where most spectators gathered. It was also easy to see that many of the riders got tired, especially galloping up and down those steep hills—so tired, in fact, that instead of being able to maintain a galloping position, up off their horse's back, some rode the course as if sitting on a chair.

Some adult amateurs, and some kids as well, aren't strong enough, or fit enough, to safely and competently ride the cross-country phase of an event, because, as the saying goes, "They run out of gas."

> We have made inactivity a habit, and the only way to break out of one habit is to create a different habit.
>
> ■ ■ ■

I know that there are a thousand-and-one reasons and excuses that we all make about why we aren't better athletes. We are parents of time-absorbing kids. We have full-time sedentary jobs. We commute two hours a day to work. We are so tired when we get home at night we have no energy left over. We are old. We are recovering from injury or illness. We just don't have the time or the energy or the whatever to do any more than we already do.

But that's not really true, except insofar as we make it true. What *is* true is that we have made inactivity a habit, and the only way to break out of one habit is to create a different habit. I call this "A Very Modest Idea" because my idea isn't to join a gym to pump iron, or to need special equipment, or to do sit-ups or pushups, or to gallop racehorses, or any of that. No, it's to start, today, by adding 15 minutes of walking to what we normally would do. That's it, nothing more. You absolutely do have, somewhere in the next 24 hours, an available 15 minutes that you would normally have spent sitting, to walk instead.

Walking means that you go for a walk, or climb the stairs in your office building instead of using the elevator, or walk down the corridor at the airport between flights, or walk around your house, or park farther away from where you work, or something to get you started on a new routine. Make yourself do this every day for a few weeks, just 15 little minutes out of the 1,440 per day. Then add five minutes. Then add five more. See where it goes. Maybe you'll walk faster at some point. Or walk up some inclines, or add more minutes, but the point is to do something more physical than you do now.

Sitting is a treacherous habit. I recently heard that "sitting is the new smoking." It ruins our athletic abilities. It ruins our health. It's not easy to change a habit. ("Habits begin as cobwebs, and end up as cables.") So don't try anything so dramatic that you know there's no way you'll keep it up. Fifteen minutes every day, that's it, for now. Three five-minute walks. Five three-minute walks. You can do this.

Long Term or Short Term, AKA "Why the Rush?"

There are definitely sports that are youth sports, gymnastics being an obvious example. Many sports that cause heavy wear and tear on knees, shoulders, and various joints see few athletes lasting very deeply into their thirties, and a 40-year-old professional football player is called "the old man."

Horseback riding definitely has the potential to be a wear-and-tear sport, but that's from falls and wrecks, not from the inherent stresses that accompany daily riding. With luck, a rider who is, say, 12, should be looking at a riding life that can easily continue for the next 40 to 50 years, and not only last for decades, but also have the prospect of being an elite riding career for many of those years.

There is a tendency for younger riders not to think in these longer-range terms, but to have the misconception that if they fail to reach some goal by, say, 25 or 30, their dreams are dashed, their riding life is washed up, and their goals must be abandoned. Partly, this is the fault of the way the various horse sports create "Youth" or "Young Rider" divisions, as though mastery weren't a continuum but a finite goal.

Perhaps there is a better way to look at the stages of a rider's career. Let's say someone starts riding at 10 or 12. Let's give them the first 10 years or so to get to be "pretty good." Not to make it to some international level, but to develop a good, independent seat, to have the start of an understanding about how horses think and react, to begin to get a handle on various emotional issues: temper, perhaps, or frustration, or impatience. Just as we might think that a 22-year-old gymnast could be entering the twilight of her sports life, so we should think of the 22-year-old rider as entering the dawn of hers.

> **Many talented young riders who later "disappear" don't lack ability, they lack staying power.**
>
> ■ ■ ■

Then the following two decades, from, say, 22 to 42, even to her late forties, will be thought of as the "heart" of her competitive riding life, and the "heart of the heart" will probably be the decade of her thirties. This is the time when there's most likely to be an intersection of drive, hunger, physical capability, emotional stability, and the years of accumulation of the necessary skill sets. A 35-year-old rider, the saying goes, is "young enough to still want it, young enough to still have the physical strength to do it, and smart enough to know how."

There are riders in their fifties, even into their sixties, like Mark Todd, who can still be competitive. Usually, it's not so much the skills that go, or even the fitness, as much as a waning of that fierce, driving "want" or need.

My point in this is to say to younger riders, and to their parents, that there's plenty of time. Plenty of time to both get a college education *and* ride. Plenty of time to bounce around well into their twenties at lower than the higher levels, and still be able to get to the top. If, however, a young rider sets an arbitrary goal, like "having" to ride at the Advanced Level by 25 or so, and if she fails to achieve that goal, here's the fear: She won't say, "Hey, so I didn't make it by (25-27-30, take your pick) so I'll recalibrate my goal to a later age." No. Instead, she's apt to think she's failed, period.

That's probably one of the reasons we see so much attrition in the ranks of younger riders. They appear on the scene, flame like a Fourth of July rocket,

Horses or College vs. Horses and College

Some high school seniors who ride will go to college or to some educational equivalent, horses or no horses. Other high school seniors never plan on any further education after high school. But for horse-loving seniors who might otherwise go on to college, it can seem tempting to skip college and go directly into some type of horse job.

Often, the parents or other advi-sors of these on-the-fence seniors will drag out all the familiar objections: "If you don't have a college degree, and something goes wrong with your horse dreams, what will you do, flip burgers at McDonald's?" Or, "All well and good, but what if you get hurt and can't ride. Then what?" And so on.

These days, though, so many colleges have riding programs that there need not be a choice between going to college and continuing with riding. Many colleges now offer riding as a varsity sport, most of these under the broad aegis of the Intercollegiate Horse Show Association (IHSA).

The choice for the horse-loving, high-school senior about college, yes, or college, no, just became a whole lot easier.

The Mount Holyoke College Equestrian Team accepting its trophy for winning the Intercollegiate Horse Show Asso-ciation (IHSA) Zone 1 Equitation Finals with coach C.J. Laws at right.

then fade and vanish. They didn't lack ability, they lacked staying power. They set goals that weren't logical, failed to meet those goals, and then felt like a failure. Certainly, this isn't the only reason they vanish. The bigger reason is that old saying, "Life gets in the way." But for those who might have had the potential to be good riders, the mistake they may have made was to think in terms of short-term goals, rather than in terms of the long-term quest toward mastery.

Stretching

I have never met a gym teacher or a physical therapist who advocates forcing a stretch. In fact, the two most common warnings you read about stretching muscles are, "Don't force a stretch," and "Don't bounce a stretch."

Muscle fibers are elastic, but only up to a point, and if forced beyond that point, they will tear, causing excruciating pain, and can easily sustain long-term damage.

You know yourself how you start to feel pain when you stretch some part of your body past its comfort zone. You also know that the way to elongate muscle fibers, to create an expanded range of motion, is to go to the place where it starts to feel uncomfortable, take it a little bit farther, hold for a few seconds, then release. Then repeat. When this is done carefully, over time, you will be able to expand how far you can take it, whether it's touching your toes, stretching tight shoulder muscles, or whatever.

Now, let's revisit stretching the horse while we're on the subject, I can't reiterate this enough. The horse can't tell us, "This is really starting to hurt me." So many riders slap their horses into draw reins, bitting rigs, leverage devices, strong bits, and crank the horse into submission, all in the name of "training."

Far better to do with the horse what you would want a personal trainer to do with you: Take the horse to what feels like the edge of his comfort zone, go a tiny bit farther, then release (fig. 5.4). Take weeks, maybe months, a little bit at a time. Never think of it in days, or God forbid, as something to be achieved in one session.

5.4: Stretching, whether by a person or a horse, can gradually elongate muscle fibers, thereby leading to an increase in range of motion. Maxim number one always applies, "Don't force a stretch."

Stretching can be a trainer's great friend or a fierce antagonist, all depending upon the feel, tact, and empathy of the trainer. Of the many ways it is possible to bring true cruelty into the realm of horse training, forcing a stretch, either down or laterally, must be one of the worst.

So just eradicate it from your system. No wiggle room here, I think.

Moving Up to a Harder Level

Many riders find a comfortable niche and stay there. Probably the majority, if we read the statistics, which show a huge base and a tiny top. I can't speak for other horse sports, but in eventing, this huge base comprises the two levels called Beginner Novice and Novice. There are levels below these not recognized by the USEA, and they are called, variously, "Grasshopper," "Green as Grass," "Minnow," and the like.

As we talked about back on page 156, by all means, if you are secure and happy and safe at one of these levels, and have no burning desire to get out of your comfort zone, just happily stay there. But there are many riders with the aspiration to climb the ladder who may be seeking some guidance about how to make the climb with a good chance of success. If so, here are a few ideas that you may find useful.

The building blocks that make up any rider and horse will include physical strength and fitness, various skill sets, emotional readiness, the requisite knowledge, and the confidence that comes when these others are solidly in place. Conversely, if some of the building blocks are either missing or deficient, then horse, rider, or both may well lack the necessary confidence. I often quote Jack Le Goff's saying about boldness and confidence (see p. 126).

"Be prepared" is more than a motto for Boy Scouts.

■ ■ ■

Getting Your Homework Done

As I told you earlier, Vince Lombardi, the Green Bay Packers football coach for whom the Super Bowl trophy is named, said, "Fatigue makes cowards of us all." Fatigue can cause rider falls. It can lead to bowed tendons, torn suspensory ligaments, and all sorts of other horse injuries. So, if you are truly serious about moving from one level to a higher and harder level, make sure that both you and your horse are both hard enough, tough enough, and fit enough to withstand the harder demands. No panting and flailing three-quarters of the way around cross-country by the rider, no "cooked" horse at the finish line. You owe this to your horse, even if you would forego it for yourself. So get out there and spend more hours in the saddle, using those long walks I introduced in chapter three to help create base fitness before gradually adding trot sets, adding hills if possible, and carefully intro-

5.5: Horses and humans are capable of tremendous exertion, but only if they have been prepared to withstand those stresses over months and, usually, years, of gradually increasing preparation. In 2004, when I finished the Tevis Cup race on Rett Butler in seventy-fifth place out of 250 starters, I had been riding for 21 hours over unrelenting terrain. It's been said of those high-tensile endurance horses, "It is like riding a miracle."

ducing faster work, as you monitor, monitor, monitor (fig. 5.5).

What skills are necessary for the new level? First, in eventing, there is basic horse care: feeding, worming, shoeing, dental care, all the prerequisite management skills. There are dressage skills. Show jumping skills. Most important, cross-country skills. Why "most important?" Because bad dressage or show jumping is embarrassing, but bad cross-country riding is dangerous. So learn how to deal with the various new demands of speed, height, complexity *at home*, before you take your new game on the road. "Be prepared" is more than a motto for Boy Scouts.

You have to know what you are doing. Knowledge can come from experience, lessons, observation, books, videos, clinics, conversations, but you need to have it. Good riders tend to simply know a lot more about all kinds of horse-related matters than lesser riders, so go study harder.

If all these pieces are in place, if you and your horse are tough, fit athletes, if you've practiced and practiced to learn the appropriate skills, and if you know what you're doing, then you will probably discover that your confidence level is high enough to take the next step, whether it's the baby step from Grasshopper to Beginner Novice, or the giant step from Intermediate to Advanced.

And always remember that in all horse sports, it's a partnership, rider and horse. So if either one of you is a weaker link, fix that first. Don't think that one can make up too much for the other. A little bit, sure, but only a little. Real trouble is just waiting when an unready rider thinks a great horse will "fill in the missing pieces," just as the great rider will need the great horse to gallop around Badminton next spring.

So do your homework, be brave, and good luck!

Build from the Base Up

There is a saying that, "If you want to build jumper riders, build them from the base up."

The base of support is not your knee. It is that part of your lower leg, right by your Achilles tendon, and part way up your calf. The only way to get that part on the horse is to soften your knee (figs. 5.6 A & B). When your knee is pinching, it will inevitably take that lower leg off to swing in the breeze to its black little heart's delight. You cannot have it both ways.

5.6 A & B: When I started jumping in 1961, I had bad basics. I jumped ahead of the motion, and my lower leg swung back toward my horse's hips. In 1975, on Sunland Scot, I was still bad (A). By the time Foxed Again came along, 20 years later, I had repaired myself (B). It is never too late to make amends.

Rett Butler

Way, way back in 1956, when I was riding Bonfire in my first GMHA 100-Mile, unbeknownst to any of us then on the East Coast, there was a 100-mile race being run for the second year in the California mountains near the town of Auburn.

Within a few years, word of this endurance race, called the Tevis Cup, had filtered back to Vermont, and a few eastern riders, including my friends Allen Leslie and Ann Alexandre, had gone out there and completed what was billed as the most difficult 100-mile one-day endurance ride in the world.

Because I have always been drawn by challenges that I half suspected I might not be able to meet, I had put the Tevis on my "bucket list," although nobody was yet using that phrase.

As nearly half a century trundled by, and I hadn't even been doing any endurance racing, far less doing any races in far off California, I began to add the Tevis Cup to things like the Maryland Hunt Cup—forever unrealized goals. But then, out of the blue, in 1998, Lana Wright invited me to ride her little Arabian gelding Zion in a 100-mile endurance race in Bethune, South Carolina. I finished that

"Bucket list" is a term for things you want to accomplish before you "kick the bucket." When I was getting Bonfire ready, in the early winter of 1955, for my first 100-mile trail ride in 1956, the first Tevis Cup in Auburn, California had just taken place. For almost half a century, I had that ride on my bucket list. In 2004, Rett Butler took me down that legendary trail.

ride after midnight, cold, shaking with fever from a bad cold, sore in every body part, and hooked on a new sport.

I started to add endurance racing on Arabians to competing in events, which eventually led to a rekindled desire to ride in the Tevis Cup. Theoretically, it is smarter and more realistic to start a tough sport like endurance racing before you reach 60, but as the kids say, you gotta do what you gotta do.

Someone told me about a little bay Arabian named Rett Butler who had already finished the Tevis Cup twice. He was for sale in Saugus, California. I flew out there, tried him, and bought him from Tammy Robinson, a seasoned endurance rider who, over the next several years, became a mentor in my new sport.

Rett Butler was not a typical Arabian. He was a stocky little bay horse, thicker in the neck, more like a little Morgan in type than one of those elegant Arabs with the long crested necks and chiseled faces. What Rett brought was fundamental and simple: Rett was game.

Over many decades, I have come to respect that one trait, being game, as the key attribute a horse can have. It is like the phrase "true grit." A game horse tries. He tries when he is tired, he keeps trying when most horses have quit trying. I will take game over talent, over elegant good looks, over brilliance, because the horse that just keeps going will still be going when those fancier horses have packed it in. That was Rett.

In Retrospect: What I'd Do Differently with Rett Butler

Each of the FEI disciplines, the main ones being dressage, show jumping, eventing, endurance, reining, and driving, is an entire body of knowledge in and of itself. And there is a saying that sometimes a person knows "just enough to be dangerous."

I would think that saying pertains to me in terms of knowing how to get horses to that razor-thin cutting edge of fitness required to excel at the highest levels of endurance racing.

If I had enough lifetimes, and if I wanted to "do right" by a horse like Rett Butler, I would spend far more time learning from the true experts. I'd want to know more about all sorts of matters: feeding, shoeing, how fast, how far, how often, how long the rest breaks, when to push, when to rest. I would want to be better than dangerous. I would want to know far more about how to do it the right way. When I bought Rett Butler from Tammy Robinson, I had the benefit of her expertise. I needed more of that.

So, number one, get the lower leg on, and that means literally touching the hair of the horse. You may well have to shorten your stirrups to allow this to happen. Many people think a long stirrup gives more support, when the opposite is likely more true. Then, instead of thinking, "upper body forward," as a way of not getting left behind, think instead "hips back" while maintaining the position of your lower leg. When your hips go back, your upper body

"Catch-22" Situations

Strictly speaking, a "Catch-22" (from the book by Joseph Heller) is "a problematic situation for which the only solution is denied by a circumstance inherent in the problem or by a rule." For example, losing something is typically a conventional problem; to solve it, you look for the lost item until you find it. But if the thing lost is your glasses, you cannot see to look for them—a Catch-22. The term "Catch-22" is also used more broadly to mean a tricky problem or a no-win or absurd situation.

In the book, Catch-22 is a military rule typifying bureaucratic operation and reasoning. The rule is not stated in a general form, but the principal example in the book fits the definition above: "If one is crazy, one does not have to fly missions; and one must be crazy to fly. But one has to apply to be excused, and applying demonstrates that one is not crazy. As a result, one must continue flying."

With horses, there are lots of Catch-22 situations.

• A horse does not carry himself in balance because he is weak behind. But he is weak behind because he does not carry himself.

• A horse is tight in his body because he does not stretch. But the horse does not stretch because he is tight in his body.

• A rider is tense and tight because the horse seems nervous and reactive. But the horse is nervous and reactive because the rider is tense.

Any time there seems to be this

has no choice but to go back, but now you will be centered in balance over the motion, instead of in front of the motion. You will sort of resemble a question mark (the stem being your lower leg).

Now think, "Raise the chin." This will flatten your back.

Now think, "Allow with arms and hands toward the bit, so as to create a fairly straight line."

sort of internal contradiction, it is the mission of the good trainer to figure out the root cause, and address that, rather than to do what trainers with fewer skills do, which is usually to blame the horse for "being bad." The lesser trainers will try to force the weak horse to lift, perhaps by using stronger aids, stronger "gear," or to bend by using leverage devices and force. Or to calm down by drilling on the horse to "make him tired enough to be obedient."

The less the trainer knows, the more apt the trainer is to address the problems incorrectly, and here is another Catch-22 situation: The "lesser" trainer does not seek education because he thinks he already knows. But the "lesser" trainer thinks he already knows, because he does not seek education.

This Morgan mare Catch A Cloud, because of her owner's health, had spent six months stall-bound. Now I am starting the slow process of building her strength and endurance.

Some trainers learn better ways, while others stay the same their whole lives through. There are too many horses in my past that need an apology from me, but in some small measure, I can try to do so by being far more patient with the ones I ride now.

Sure, this seems like a lot of fuss, but it's why they invented practice.

Equitation is not for appearance. That is secondary to creating security and balance and structural integrity of the various body parts of the rider.

Ask yourself this simple question, "Who would I rather resemble, Bill Steinkraus or a flying sack of garbage?"

Hey, whichever floats your boat!

When in doubt: lean forward, look down, pinch with the knees, let your lower leg slip back, throw your upper body up the neck, and yell "jump!"

> If you ask for something and the answer is "no" you are no worse off than if you had never asked.
>
> ■ ■ ■

Funny, yes? Then why is it so blasted instinctive?

When I started jumping back in the 1960s, I had no clue about how *not* to do this.

This position has a million flaws, and it is worse than simply being ugly and unbalanced. It makes the rider weak and insecure, and it unbalances the horse and leaves him to his own devices as to whether to jump or not, because the driving aid of the lower leg is nonexistent.

Gradually, I learned how to repair these posture aberrations.

"No for an Answer I Already Got"—Old Yiddish Saying

Door-to-door sales people live or die by this truth. If you ask for something and the answer is "no" you are no worse off than if you had never asked.

But sometimes the answer is yes.

I've ridden a lot of horses that I did not own but had probably asked to ride, or at any rate, made it known that I would like to ride. And so I got to ride dozens of nice horses, year after year, and got enormous amounts of riding mileage without having to pay to get it (figs. 5.7 A & B).

If you want to ride more horses, you absolutely have to get over your fear of rejection, and ask. Plenty of times, the answer will be, "No," or, "Thanks, but I have someone else to ride this one," or some similar no for an answer, but you already had that before you asked.

5.7 A & B: Don't be afraid to ask to ride nice horses. The worst they can say is "no." There are wonderful horses just sitting out there, waiting just for you. I asked, and got to ride Dapper Dan (A) and Ramegwa Sharli (B), two of my all-time favorites. What if I had been too timid to ask?

5.8: Jack Le Goff used to say that the key to a good canter is to figure out how to "mesh" two incompatible qualities—balance and impulsion—in the same canter. Ever since, I have relied upon this advice as a cornerstone of my training strategies.

Sometimes the answer might not be a straight "Yes," but it may be along the lines of, "I don't have a horse for you to ride, but I know Sally has one she needs to get ridden."

You can't get to be a better rider without riding. It is a type of Catch-22, in that you need more riding hours in order to get better, but you need to be better before you are offered horses to ride. So do an end run and ask anyway. I wasn't any good when I wheedled many of those early rides, but I faked it pretty well.

Be brave. Dare rejection. What the hell— "No for an answer I already got." So what if they say no? You are no worse off than if you hadn't asked.

6

Rider Knowledge

What You Know

The American humorist Will Rogers said it best, "Everyone is ignorant, only about different subjects."

No one can know all there is to know about horses. It is far too wide and too diverse a world. Most people only know about the part of the horse world they inhabit, and even then, most have gaps in their knowledge. So don't get too stressed about all the horse-related subjects you don't know about, because it is inevitable. As Rogers said, ignorance is normal.

Do realize, though, that you can always acquire more knowledge any time you are so inclined, from experience, from books, from movies and videos, from clinics and lessons, and from just talking with other horse people.

There are some things about horses that most horse people know, like how to lead a horse, how to put on a saddle, how to mount, how to steer and stop, very basic basics. Then there are facts that are totally breed- or discipline-specific. A Thoroughbred breeder will know who Nasrullah was, and a Morgan breeder will know about Upwey Ben Don, but few people will know about both of those breed-shaping stallions. A dressage rider will know that a 10-meter circle at E or B touches X, and a jumper rider knows that the distance between two fences in a one-stride in-and-out is about 24 feet.

Most horse people know that when you unload a horse from a trailer you untie the horse's head before you take down the butt bar, so that is "general" knowledge. Each breed of horse or pony will have lore and legend about how the breed developed, who the breed-shaping horses were, and how this breed differs from other breeds. Each breed has all sorts of rules and regulations and standards and requirements and breeding and registration policies.

> Knowledge about horses is like a giant lake, and you can drink and drink and drink, and you won't make much of a dent in the lake.
>
> ■ ■ ■

Every riding and driving discipline comes with a vast body of knowledge specific to what is done, or not done, as it pertains to that specific horse sport. Rules that apply to show hunters may not apply to endurance horses or cutting horses, although some might.

All horses have a skeleton, a respiratory system, a cardiovascular system, and parts of the body that are the same regardless of breed or size or intended use.

So pick your fights, so to speak, because knowledge about horses is like a giant lake, and you can drink and drink and drink, and you won't make much of a dent in the lake.

On the other hand, why be what George Morris calls a "dum dum," when, with some study, you can be a "smart smart"?

It's out there, that lake. Do you sip or do you gulp? That part is up to you.

In the following sections are some little sips of knowledge, and perhaps some strategies about ways to take bigger gulps.

I hope you are thirsty!

How Good a Rider Do You Want to Be?

As I've mentioned, I wrote an entire book on this subject; it's called *How Good Riders Get Good,* and that's where to go for more in-depth analysis.

But here I *will* say that how good someone wants to be is often more in that person's control than most of us think. Barring circumstances like illness, injury, age (past a certain point), being in jail, or other unfortunate realities, getting good depends on how badly you want it, and what you are willing to sacrifice in order to get it.

Drive, passion, commitment, perseverance, grit, courage, yadda, yadda, yadda—I know you have heard all that 20 million times, so what else is new?

Not much. The reason these platitudes are spouted is because most of the good ones have more of those qualities than most of the bad ones. Which is partly bad news and partly good news.

> Getting good depends on how badly you want it and what you are willing to sacrifice in order to get it.
>
> ◼ ◼ ◼

The bad news is that it is a pain in the you know what to have to work that hard. The good news is that it's possible—if you do work that hard.

"I don't have time." Yes, you do. You have to give up other stuff. "Like what?" You know, family, dating, financial security, a home, pets, eating out, stuff like that. "I don't have enough money." Right, you don't. Unless you were born rich. So you will need to work at a barn doing scut work in order to be able to ride more horses. You need to ride horses.

"I don't want to give up my life. I don't want a cruddy job mucking stalls. I want to get to be a good rider, but I want to have a normal life." See my prior answer. You should have been born rich.

Good riders get to be good riders, and then better riders, by riding and riding and riding and riding and riding. If you can figure out how to do that, your future as a better rider is assured. If you can't, you won't.

Victor Dakin

I n the early spring of 1973, May and I were living in Strafford, Vermont. Our first son, Rett, was four months old, and I was a real-estate broker with a small firm called Strafford Associates. We had two horses in the old green barn next to our house, Cat and House Guest, and I had ridden both of them in a few Advanced events, but in terms of being or even becoming an "international" three-day rider, I wasn't on anyone's radar.

It was an okay life. I didn't get up each morning dreading the day, but neither did I feel particularly excited about my work. Henry David Thoreau famously said something to the effect that "most men live lives of quiet desperation." I was far from that, but at the age of 31, I still felt that there had to be more to life than driving people around to see houses and farms. It was as if I were treading water.

Then one day, out of nowhere, came a letter from Woodstock, Vermont, from a young woman named Jane Schemilt, a student at the Doscher School of Photography up Morgan Hill Road from GMHA. I had met Jane at various events where she was riding her little plain bay horse, Victor Dakin, but I didn't know her well, nor had I paid much more than glancing attention to Victor. Jane said, in the letter, that since she was going to become a full-time medical photographer, she had made the sad decision to sell Victor. Would I be interested in him? Why she wrote me instead of one of many other riders, I do not know. What I do know is that Jane's letter, and our subsequent decision to buy Victor Dakin, changed the entire trajectory of my life.

At first, during the spring and summer of 1973, I wondered if I had made a big mistake, because as far as dressage was concerned, I couldn't, as the saying goes, "ride one-half of him." Victor was hot, reactive, and nervous. When Jane had ridden him in a Canadian team tryout the prior season, the Canadian coach had exclaimed, "This bloody horse can't canter," and it was true that in the small confines of a 20-by-60-meter dressage ring, he was explosive.

Forty-three years later, I can't remember what events I rode him in first, but in September of 1973, Neil Ayer was putting on the first Ledyard International Three-Day Event, in Wenham,

A gold-medal horse can change the entire trajectory of your life. Here's Victor Dakin on cross-country at the 1974 USET World Championships at Burghley, England, on his way to a team gold medal.

Massachusetts, and had actually paid the air transport so that top European riders would come to compete there. I entered Victor, largely unprepared, lacking in all sorts of riding skills, but fueled by the conviction that it was pretty much now or never. I was, I now realize, in over my head in some ways, but Victor's strengths largely made up for my failings.

I made the mistake on cross-country of "hand riding" Victor, trying to set him up in front of his jumps, instead of attacking them and letting Victor set

himself up, and we had two refusals on the course. But we finished. And we now had an entire winter to get to know one another before a series of World Championship selection trials to be held in the spring of 1974 to select six riders to train in England with the new USET coach, Jack Le Goff, prior to the World Championships at Burghley in September.

All that cold winter of 1973 and 1974, I boarded Victor at Huntington Farm, a couple of miles up the road in Strafford, and we plugged away in that dark, cold,

(continued)

Victor Dakin (continued)

60-by-120-foot indoor ring. But when it is 10 below zero outside, with 3 feet of snow on the level, that ring seemed huge and warm by comparison.

When May and Victor and I headed south in May and June to try to make the USET squad of nine riders to train at the new headquarters on Bridge Street in South Hamilton, Massachusetts, I had learned the one single most critical thing about how to ride Victor over jumps. I had to trust him, ride him forward, keep my leg on, stay out of his way, and he would explode off the ground in all his attack mode.

For the next five years, Victor never had a refusal on any cross-country course in the world.

Because we had been consistent at the selection trials, I was one of nine riders to be invited for a month or so of training at the USET, at the end of which Jack Le Goff would choose six of us to get on the plane to England. Eventually, four would make up the actual team, and the other two would ride as individuals.

The original nine were the two veterans, Mike Plumb and Bruce Davidson, plus Beth Perkins, Caroline Treviranus, Don Sachey, Roger Haller, Tad Coffin, Lornie Forbes, and myself.

I had few illusions. I was married, with a full-time job and a son. I was absolutely not what Jack wanted, someone to live at the Team in South

THE GLITTER OF GOLD
AMERICAN TEAM
SWEEPS WORLD CHAMPIONSHIPS

BY FIFI COLES

Our American team, which for many years has been shining with silver, is now glittering with gold. Bruce Davidson riding his own Ir[...]ap won the individual World Championship title and the FEI Gold Medal, while our Team finished with a resounding victory o[...]ine other countries to capture the team Gold.

That spirits ran high after this victory is undeniably true. Indeed it was a very special victory. We left the United States for England [...]uly with seven Grade 1 horses. As only ten horses, competing at the advanced level were available to Jack LeGoff, it might be s[...]hat we took just about all we had.

From a pinto pony in a backyard converted chicken coop in Greenfield, Massachusetts, in 1952, to the gold medal at the World Championships in Burghley, England, 22 years later, seems an improbable journey.

Hamilton under his constant direction, the way we associate with professional athletes in sports like baseball and football. I figured that I was ninth out of nine, and that I had four weeks to prove that, like the line in the Beatles' song, we had "a ticket to ride."

We continued to struggle in dressage, but Victor Dakin was proving to be a jumping machine. I didn't have all the skills that I later learned, but if I left it up to him, Victor would attack the cross-country, and leave the rails in their cups in show jumping.

We got on the plane.

In England, Victor's jumping was consistently perfect, and we were chosen to be one of the four members of the American team. Victor jumped a clear cross-country round, and he was one of the three U.S. horses whose final results gave us a gold medal. I remember Prince Philip handing me my medal, and saying, "Well done, boys."

The impossible had become improbable, the improbable had become possible, and the possible had become reality.

From that day forward, I could make my living in the horse business, so totally can a gold medal horse change your life.

In Retrospect: What I'd Do Differently with Victor Dakin

Victor Dakin, much like Cat, was afraid of flatwork. I had been told that one of the reasons that Victor's previous rider had not been chosen for the Canadian Olympic squad was that the coach did not like Victor.

Just as I now realize what I should have done with Cat, I should also have tried with Victor Dakin—that is, all sorts of strategies to try to win his confidence and alleviate his almost claustrophobic fear of being placed between the driving aids and the restraining aids.

I think my approach would have been hours of walking, trying to get him to stretch and bend without any fear of force or coercion.

"You don't know what you don't know."

I would get frustrated by Victor's tension and resistance, and, in my ignorant frustration, would respond with equal tension, not knowing that I was only making matters worse.

The Perennial Debate: Talent vs. Work Ethic

There are those with so much innate riding talent "it would make the angels weep," but if they are shirkers instead of workers, usually that talent goes to waste. Others with little talent struggle relentlessly for years, yet never achieve their dreams. So it's pretty obvious that neither talent alone nor work ethic alone is sufficient to propel a person to the top echelons of their chosen field.

But if I had to choose one—a supremely gifted rider with a modest work ethic, or a fanatically hard worker, possessed of moderate talent—I'd bet on the worker. Thomas Edison said, "Genius is one percent inspiration, 99 percent perspiration." Workers create talent, through relentless practice, where talent didn't formerly exist. Hang around any barn, and watch. There are those who could hustle and get in another horse or two before lunch, but who have an amazing ability to stall around. They head off for leisurely lunch hours that turn into two hours, and when the day is done, the hustler back at the barn has ridden six or seven horses to the two or three of the leisure lover.

Now multiply that by a month, a year, a decade, and the hard worker is well on the way to that 10,000 hours postulated by Malcolm Gladwell in his book *Outliers* as the magical entry requirement to huge success.

When I wrote *How Good Riders Get Good*, for which Sandra Cooke interviewed 24 of the world's best riders and drivers, I actually expected that hard work would be just one of the pieces of what they thought had enabled them to get good. Turns out it was the biggest piece. There are thousands and thousands of riders who weekly spend $50 and more for riding lessons to, presumably, either "get good" or at least get better, but not that many of them have bothered to work hard enough to actually read what those great riders had to say.

I'd say it's the intellectual study of riding that so many avoid. There is physical laziness, but there is also intellectual laziness, and either one is a dream wrecker.

Many barn owners will tell the same sad tale. They tell the riders at their barn that if they will help out, especially on weekends, they can ride extra horses. Now very often these riders will look you right in the eye and passionately declare how much they "want it," but when these riders are given the choice of working off extra riding hours or doing something else, most barn owners can tell you what choice they will make.

There is physical laziness, but there is also intellectual laziness, and either one is a dream wrecker.

Hard work is hard. It's often unpleasant. It's tiring physically and mentally and emotionally. There's just that one thing, though. It so often pays off. In the 50 years I've taught riding, it's almost always been the relentless workers (who also had talent) who got it done. Which leads to this final point: If people really have passion, then working toward that passion may not really be work at all. It's just what they want to do anyway, and how lucky for them is that?

General Considerations: In Conclusion

I am not a fan of false modesty. "How did you do at the show?" you ask, fishing for the other person to tell you how they did, hopefully to be followed by them asking, "And how did you do?" which allows you to blush, look down, shrug your shoulders in an "aw shucks" gesture, and reply, "I won Champion Hunter of the Open Division."

So when I say what I am going to say, I mean it.

There is nothing about anything in this book that some specialist somewhere has not explained better, more accurately, or with more insight. "There is nothing new under the sun. Under the sun, there is nothing new." What I have tried to do in *Know Better to Do Better* is to trace a personal journey, to come at common situations that we find with horses and riders from various directions, and diverse viewpoints, and to point toward ways and means to get better by knowing more.

If you want a magical adventure, go read Walter Farley's *The Black Stallion*. You won't be disappointed.

Lightning Magic

By the summer of 1961, I had been involved with Morgan horses for eight years, since first spectating at the 1953 National Morgan Show. I was working at the Green Mountain Stock Farm in Randolph, Vermont, during my summer break between sophomore and junior year at Dartmouth College.

Allen Leslie called me and said that he was going down to Hamilton, Massachusetts, to watch some type of competition called three-day eventing, and did I want to come?

I got Art Titus, the head Morgan trainer, to give me the weekend off, and Allen and I drove to a farm called Groton House, where a championship called the Wofford Cup was being held. For the first time, I watched cross-country galloping and jumping. Jumping down steep slides, jumping over huge mounds, jumping into the Ipswich River, and it was as though a giant light bulb went off in my head.

I wanted to do it, because I didn't know how to do it, and up to that point I thought that I was a superb rider. It challenged that cocky assumption, and I didn't like that.

Back at work training Morgans on Monday morning in Randolph, I asked Art Titus, "Hey, Art. How do you learn to jump?"

Art's reply was pure and simple genius. "Put up a jump one foot high and jump it until you get bored. Then raise it."

This is precisely what Aristotle said about learning by doing, and it was the way I tended to learn, so that fall, back at college, I asked Joe McLaughlin at nearby Hitching Post Farm in South Royalton to teach me how to jump.

I spent most weekends at Hitching Post, riding all sorts of camp horses, and by the spring of 1962, I concluded that I needed a Thoroughbred event horse so that I could start to get ready to win a gold medal for the United States Equestrian Team. I actually thought that.

Switching from Morgans to Thoroughbreds wasn't because I had stopped liking Morgans. It was because in my new plan (to win a gold medal), Thoroughbreds were better suited to make it happen.

Lightning Magic was only five years old when I bought him from Henry and Janet Schurink in the spring of 1962. He

My first Thoroughbred, Lightning Magic, five years old when I bought him in 1962, opened so many doors. I evented him, rode him in fox hunts, raced him in point-to-points, showed him as a hunter at Ox Ridge, showed him as a jumper all over New England. I did not know enough then to understand the magnitude of the gifts that horse gave me. This photo was taken at a three-day event at GMHA in 1962.

(continued)

If you want better control over your own riding body, read Sally Swift's *Centered Riding*.

For more insight into upper-level show jumping, read books by William Steinkraus and George Morris.

When I say what I am going to say, I mean it.

■ ■ ■

There are books and books, and if you can't find what you need in one book, try another.

So, whether you sip or gulp, there ought to be something here that resonates in some way. Perhaps that will lead you to look further and to want to learn more. Have no fear on this score. If you want to dig deeper, there are many resources to help you along your journey.

Lightning Magic (continued)

was a 16.1 bay gelding by Grey Flares out of Blue Witch, foaled in 1957 in Shelburne, Vermont. Somehow I had learned that a Mr. Henri van Schaik, a former Dutch Olympic team jumping silver medalist at the 1936 Olympics in Berlin, had a farm in Cavendish, only seven miles from my parents' farm in South Reading. I arranged to train with him. Our goal was the Preliminary three-day event at GMHA, just a couple of months away.

How we made this happen—to take a green event rider and a five-year-old green event horse, and finish nineteenth out of 30 at a 12-mile-long three-day event—remains a mystery to this day, but we did.

In the spring of 1963, I was keeping Lightning Magic at the farm of my friend Judy Barwood, across the Connecticut River from Hanover, New Hampshire, where I was a senior. I had made the decision to teach sixth grade at the Far Hills Country Day School in New Jersey, because the United States Equestrian Team's headquarters were right around the corner, in Gladstone. I had not, perhaps, heard the expression, "In for a penny, in for a pound," but if I was going to get on the USET, I figured I'd better find out what that quest involved.

So off we went, Lightning Magic and I, to New Jersey. I hunted him

And Where Do We Go From Here?

With many of the horses I've ridden, I wish I could have a "do over." There are truths I once accepted that I have since learned to question and sometimes reject. There are many training strategies I used to use that I now do differently. And yet, for all of that, this isn't a book of regret or self-blame.

I think that we do the best we can with what we know. Later, when we know more, we should be able to do better.

Here's the thing I realize about the saying, "I wish I had known then

with the Essex Foxhounds, rode him in a point-to-point race, rode in the Essex Hunter Trials, evented him at the Preliminary level at events in Virginia and Maryland, and gradually began to get some grasp on how to jump and do dressage.

In Retrospect: What I'd Do Differently with Lightning Magic

Where to even begin? Basically with Lightning Magic, it was the case of "the halt leading the blind," because he was green, and we were trying to learn together, and that is a pretty good formula for the way not to do it.

I had a (sort of) independent seat, from all my years of riding bareback, but I was clueless about jumping. My stirrups were too long, I had no eye for a distance. I had no inkling of what was meant by an "adjustable canter." I jumped ahead of the motion, my lower leg slipped back, and when I look at those photos of me jumping 55 years ago, I think that it is a wonder that Lightning Magic ever jumped for me at all, because I was totally clueless.

There is a true saying, "You don't know what you don't know," and that describes me with that game horse. So if I had a do-over button with Lightning Magic, all I know is that I would push it time after time.

what I know now." The word "now" is forever receding into the past. The "now" as I write this will be a "then" when you read it.

When we say, "I wish I'd known then what I know now," that should be an optimistic statement, not one of self-flagellation, because it means that we learned and changed.

If I were to rewrite this book some years from now, I hope that I'd *need* to rewrite it because I would have kept on learning even better ways. That's why I won't conclude with the words "The End." These two words presume that my learning is over, but tomorrow, I'll climb on some horse who will show me I've still got lots to learn (fig. 6.1).

6.1: In 2018, I have a string of horses that includes two Morgan mares, High Brook Rockstar, seen in this photo, and Catch a Cloud; two Warmblood full sisters, Beaulieu's Cool Concorde and Beaulieu's Cool Attitude; and three OTTBs, Meet In Khartoum, Portada, and Tense. When anyone asks me which of all the hundreds of horses was or is my "favorite," my stock answer is, "This one that I am riding, right here, right now."

Recommended Reading

Some of Denny Emerson's favorite books, both horse-related, and non, for young and old:

Assault On Lake Casitas **by Brad Alan Lewis** (CreateSpace)

The Black Stallion **Series and** *The Island Stallion* **Series by Walter Farley** (Yearling)

The Boys in the Boat **by Daniel James Brown** (Penguin Books)

Everest: The West Ridge **by Thomas S. Hornbein** (Mountaineers Books)

Hey Cowboy, Wanna Get Lucky? **by Baxter Black** (Penguin Books)

Justin Morgan Had a Horse **by Marguerite Henry** (Aladdin)

The Making of the Modern Warmblood **by Christopher Hector** (Sporthorse International)

Sand **by Will James** (Mountain Press Publishing)

The Tevis Cup **by Marnye Langer** (The Lyons Press)

Acknowledgments

To Anne Adams, for her immense help in pulling together the many and varied segments of this book.

To May Emerson, for all the typing and encouragement.

To Trafalgar Square Books: My publisher and editor, Caroline Robbins, who has exhibited spectacular patience and meticulous attention to detail. Martha Cook, Managing Director, for years of advice and support (and for fun Morgan conversation).

Index